Mute Vol 2 #1 - KNOWLEDGE COMMONS >>

ABOUT MUTE VOL 2

Mute Vol 2 is a new imprint from the publishers of *Mute* magazine, http://metamute.org

As well as making writing from the *Mute* website and archive available in print, *Mute* Vol 2 will feature special issues, projects and readers, collecting texts from *Mute* and elsewhere.

We invite you to respond to the articles and continue the debates printed here on our website. You can contribute in the following ways: post news and articles; respond to articles; post events or announcements to our calendar; start or join in discussion threads; upload reviews or share files through our Public Library; or you can submit article proposals to the editors by contacting us at <mute@metamute.org>

MUTE ON DEMAND

Mute is printed using 'print on demand' technology and copies can be ordered for resale (or potlach re-distribution!) through the *Mute* website.

Mute can be quickly and cheaply printed for events, meetings, discussions, teaching programmes, and sundry gatherings. Editions can be as small or as large as you like, from 1 copy upwards. We offer a discount of 30% on bulk orders for resale.

Contact us for more details.
Email: <orders@metamute.org>

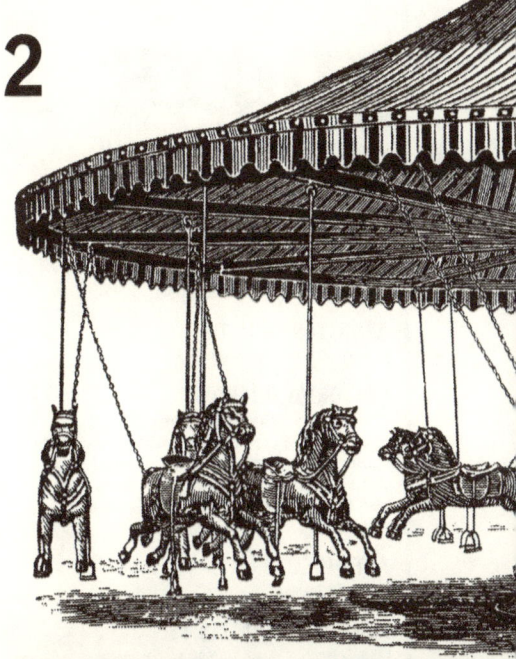

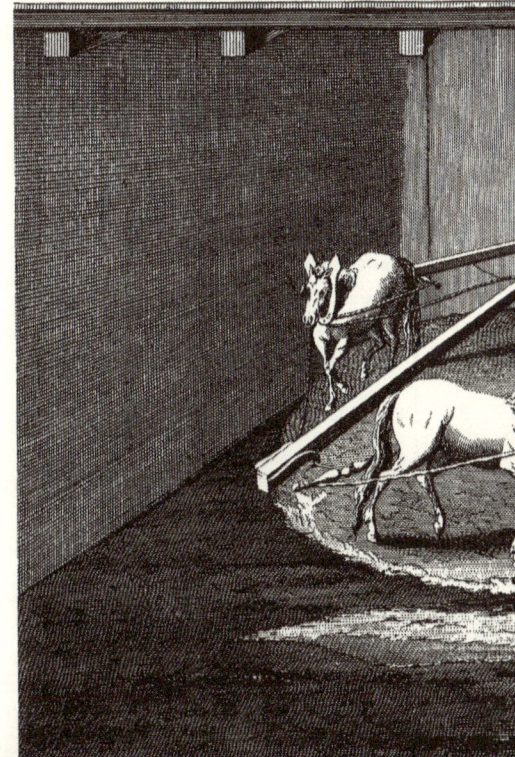

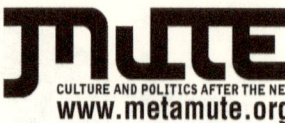

CULTURE AND POLITICS AFTER THE NET
www.metamute.org

EDITOR
Josephine Berry Slater <josie@metamute.org>

DEPUTY EDITOR
Benedict Seymour <ben@metamute.org>

ASSISTANT EDITOR
Anthony Iles <anthony@metamute.org>

EDITORIAL BOARD
Josephine Berry Slater, Matthew Hyland <convolute@riseup.org>, JJ King <jamie@jamie.com>, Demetra Kotouza <demetra@inventati.org>, Hari Kunzru <hari@metamute.org>, Pauline van Mourik Broekman, Benedict Seymour, Laura Sullivan <alchemical44@yahoo.co.uk> and Simon Worthington

ART DIRECTOR
Simon Worthington

DESIGN PRODUCTION
Laura Oldenbourg <laura_oldenbourg@yahoo.com>

ACKNOWLEDGEMENTS
Special thanks to: Per Wizén for his images *Untitled (Carousel)* and *The Hunt (after Uccello)*. Courtesy of Brändström & Stene Stockholm. Thanks to: Anja Kirschner <amk@supernumeraries.org> for the images in this issue taken from her forthcoming film *Pollyll: plan for a revolution in docklands*, http://linkme2.net/5z; Jörg Baach and Stephan Karpischek (the POD guys) for PDF wizardry; Finn Smith and Zara Hughes for all their help

The design of this edition is based on a design template orginated for *Mute* magazine by Damian Jaques <damian@aant.co.uk> of AANTGraphicDesign

ADVERTISING
<advertising@metamute.org>

WEBSITE
www.metamute.org is powered by Drupal and CiviCRM FLOSS Software, with additional software services by our very own OpenMute http://openmute.org. With thanks to Raquel Perez de Eulate and Darron Broad

OPENMUTE
CTO: Darron Broad <darron@kewl.org>; technology design: Simon Worthington; interactive and graphic design: Raquel Perez de Eulate <raquel@photofever.net> and Laura Oldenbourg

PUBLISHERS
Pauline van Mourik Broekman <pauline@metamute.org>
Simon Worthington <simon@metamute.org>

OFFICE
Mute, Unit 9, The Whitechapel Centre,
Myrdle Street,
London E1 1HL, UK
T: +44 (0)20 7377 6949
F: +44 (0)20 7377 9520
e-mail: <mute@metamute.org>

SUBSCRIPTIONS
T: +44 (0)20 7377 6949
F: +44 (0)20 7377 9520
e-mail: <subs@metamute.org>
web: http://www.metamute.org/subs/

DISTRIBUTION UK
Central Books,
99 Wallis Road,
London, E4 5LN.
T: +44 (0)20 8986 4854
F: +44 (0)20 8533 5821

CONTRIBUTING
Mute welcomes contributions of all kinds: articles, visuals or collaborations. Please email <mute@metamute.org> with your suggestions or visit metamute.org where you can post news, events and comments or contribute to the Mute Public Library.

The views expressed in *Mute* and Metamute are not necessarily those of the publishers or service providers.
Mute is published in the UK by Mute Publishing Ltd. and printed by http://lightningsource.com online digital print on demand (POD) services in the USA and UK

Cover: Per Wizén, *Untitled (Carousel)*

Mute is supported by The Arts Council of England

ARTS COUNCIL ENGLAND

ISBN: 0-9550664-1-7

MUTE VOL 2 #1 CONTENTS

WHEN AMERICA SNEEZES...

Amidst current fears over the avian influenza pandemic, the protection of human life and the protection of Intellectual Property (IP) is hanging in the balance. In the event of a global emergency, nations who have signed the WTO's draconian TRIPS agreement would not be able to afford to buy enough of the patented flu vaccine – Roche's Tamiflu – to protect their populations. They would then be forced to issue compulsory licences allowing them to produce the drug en masse without consent from the patent holder. Were this to happen, it would represent a rare and temporary moment of leniency in the relentless programme of enclosures currently being erected around ideas and intellectual 'goods' within the knowledge economy.

Whatever one thinks of the geopolitics of the avian flu scare (convenient source of distraction in the midst of current account deficits and foreign misadventures?; anti-Chinese and anti-immigrant propaganda?), it would seem to take the threat of mega-deaths in the first world to dent the regime of enclosures. As their manufacturing dwindles to an all time low and the Asian tigers threaten to become, in the words of Tessa Jowell, 'larger exporter[s] than Europe', the US, UK and other 'post-industrial' economies are placing a desperate faith in IP protection and the ability for creativity to 'add value'.

In defiance of this latter day regime of enclosures, a struggle is ensuing to produce and protect what is being called the Knowledge Commons. The idea is that, as with the pre-capitalist common lands on which the majority of people subsisted, we can build a resource, a life source, of intellectual wealth to sustain people within informatic capitalism. Promoting digital abundance and the spectre of sharing, the cyber-commoners range from libertarian capitalists promoting innovation with some rights reserved, to class struggle anarchists seeking an abolition of property without reserve. All agree that the knowledge commons must be extended and defended.

But this endeavour is not without problems, political, tactical and philosophical. In this first issue of the new format *Mute,* we have tried to foreground the antagonisms which the Knowledge Commons throw up: How does the ideal of voluntary collaborative production, exemplified by Free/Libre Open Source Software (FLOSS), connect to the incorporation of 'free labour' within post-fordist production (see our FLOSS producer's questionnaire, p.10)? How does the logic of copyleft, which turns copyright licensing on its head and which is widely used to protect the

Knowledge Commons from commercial enclosure, tackle the Law's inherent violence and arbitrariness (see Martin Hardie, p.54)? How do commons in their 'immaterial' informatic form relate to the material struggles of the world's soil-tilling majority, and are knowledge workers really the vanguard of anti-capitalism (answers can be gleaned from texts by Steve Wright, p.34, and Peter Linebaugh, p.72)? What kind of an economic resource is intellectual wealth, and does the focus on a free and fertile Knowledge Commons ultimately mirror the unqualified faith placed in the knowledge economy's ability to produce value (Steve Wright again, and Soenke Zehle, p.22)? These questions build critically on *Mute*'s earlier investigation of the 'digital commons' in 2002 – Vol 1, issue 20.

To 'produce' the working class, argues Peter Linebaugh, use-value had to be eclipsed by exchange-value and the agrarian commons bulldozed to smooth the passage of global trade. Perhaps today, the fight to defend the mutating contemporary commons in all its forms (from natural resources to indigenous knowledges) is producing a new mutant global class whose solidarities cross social strata: 'strange loops... odd circuits and strange connections between and among various class sectors' – as Midnight Notes once put it (Steve Wright, p.34). We may live to see these loops intensify, if we survive the bird flu that is. ⟍

Josephine Berry Slater <josie@metamute.org>

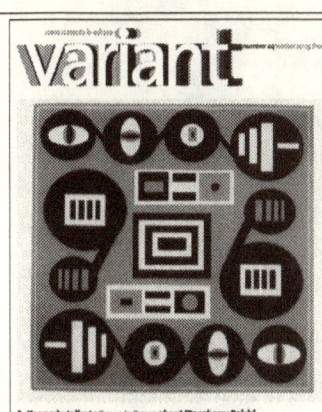

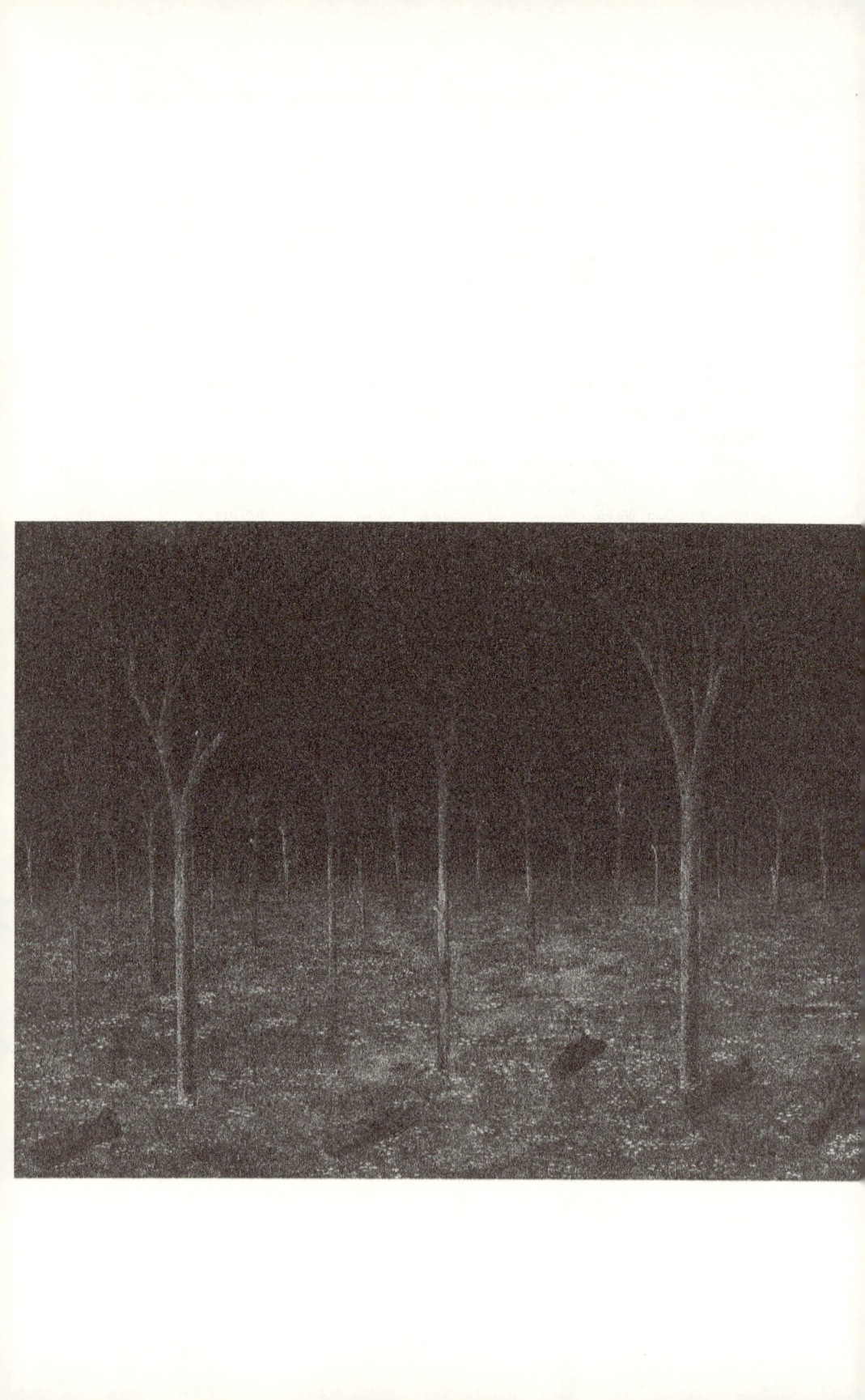

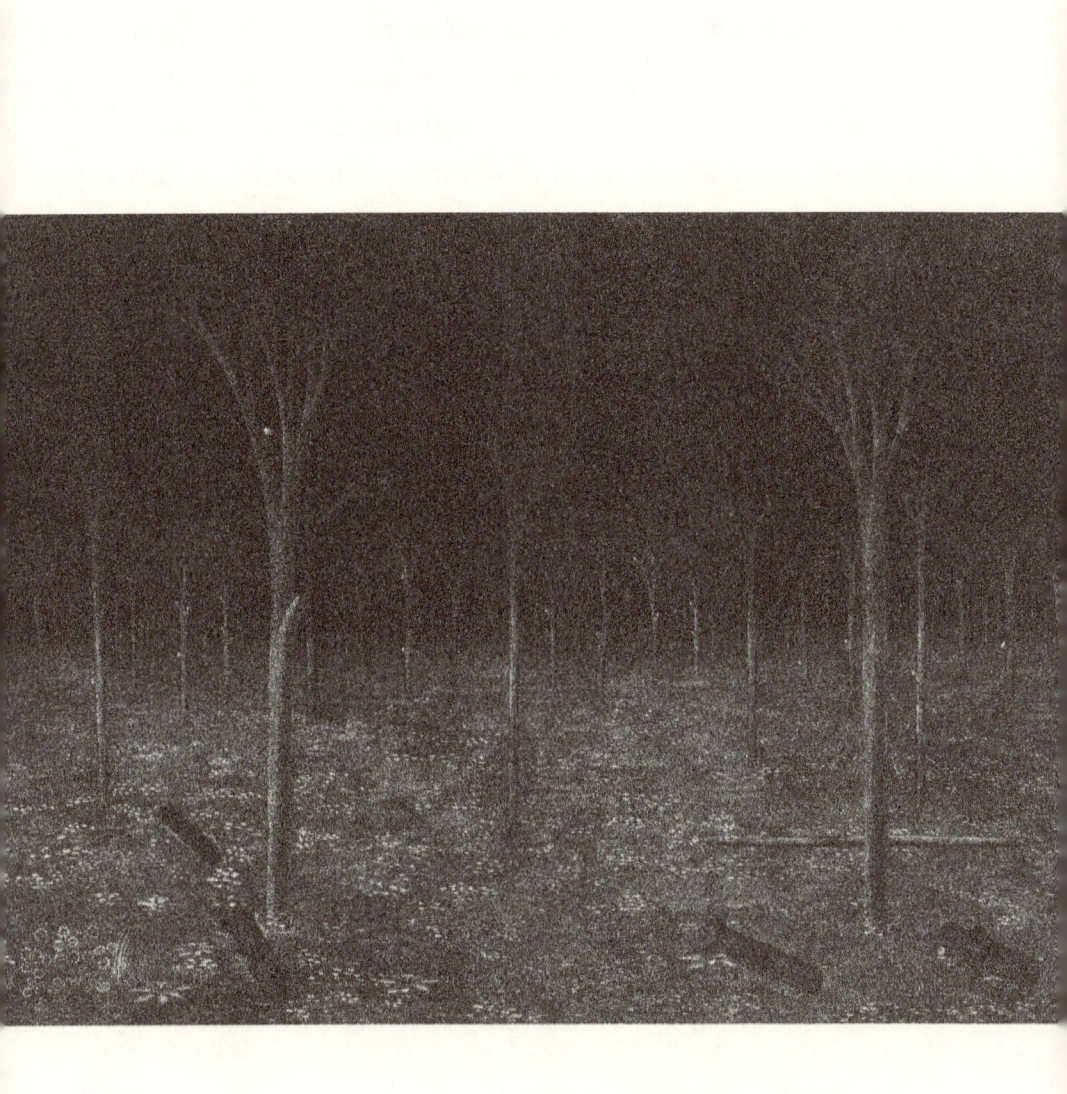

Image ❯ Per Wizén, *The Hunt (after Uccello)*, 2005, 140X380cm,
cibachrome, Courtesy Brändström & Stene Stockholm

FREE LABOUR OR SOCIAL SCULPTURE?

If the production and dissemination of Free/Libre Open Source Software (FLOSS) is a social movement, then what is its constituency and what is it fighting for? Is FLOSS a harbinger of communism, a new form of commons, or the avant garde of capitalism? *Mute* **canvassed a small but varied selection of cultural producers about the role and significance of FLOSS in their projects**

Your Name: James Wallbank
Name of Organisation: Access Space
Location: Sheffield
Website: http://access.lowtech.org/
Email: rti@lowtech.org
Recent Projects: The Linux Open Source Sound Project (LOSS): http://access.lowtech.org/loss/; Tools + Techniques 3 (Software talks): http://access.lowtech.org/events/tools+techs3/

1. What is your organisation's mission?
Access Space provides an open access media lab where people learn, create and communicate. We only use FLOSS and what we like to call 'trailing edge technology' – late model computers which other organisations feel are redundant, just because they can't run the latest version of Windows.

2. What role does FLOSS play in your organisation's economy?
FLOSS saves Access Space around £20K per annum in hardware and software costs. It's obvious how we make software savings – but just as important are the savings we make in hardware. Access Space only uses recycled computers which we can recover for nothing.
Typically, we use computers which are three to five years old. Interestingly, a recent government report on free, open source software suggests that, if you are committed to a continuous policy of software upgrades, Linux effectively DOUBLES the life of a computer.

3. Which communities do you support and how?
Our regular participants are mainly from the Sheffield area. Now we're working with eight UK organisations to spread the Access Space 'Free, Open Source Software, Recycled Hardware/Skill-Sharing Community' model.

4. How do you participate within the production of code or how do you see your role within the FLOSS ecology?
We don't see our role as code production. In fact, we do produce code snippets occasionally, and we are currently working with a local open source software consultancy, Hypercube Systems, to develop accounting software. Our real, 'Value Added' contributions to the Open Source meme are demonstration and advocacy. We run complex network systems in a difficult, real world environment (a multi-user network with constantly changing client machines) and we talk about it. Our network is robust and effective (more than can be said for many), and could be used in a variety of lab and community circumstances.

I think it's really, REALLY important that the open source community acknowledges that coding is just a part of spreading the model. Look at Microsoft – they wouldn't be in the dominant position they're in if coders were their only employees! They also employ advocates, lobbyists, educators, market researchers, advertisers, demonstrators, distributors, bug-checkers, trainers, support technicians, customer relations wonks and many more. For FLOSS to really change the world (it is already, and it will even more so!) all of these roles need to be played.

5. Do you see your work/labour as resisting, in symbiosis with, or exploited by capitalist production?
The wider 'Free Culture' movement, of which open source Software is one instance, actually starts to make this sort of terminology obsolete. Terms like 'capitalist production' tend to assume a model in which scarcity is closely linked with value – whereas in the digital and cultural realm, abundance (even ubiquity) are more closely linked to value, in a circumstance in which there are, potentially, huge surpluses of resources.

6. What are the primary obstacles you face?
None that aren't visibly eroding as we speak!

7. What licence, if any, do you use?
We like the GPL, and we like Creative Commons Attribution/Share-Alike licences, which are very similar to the GPL. We're slightly sceptical about 'non-commercial', which can restrict exciting opportunities for artists (and others) to use software and make a living.

8. Do you see yourself as contributing to a commons?
Absolutely!

Your Name: Aymeric Mansoux
Name of Organisation: GOTO10
Location: N/A
Website: http://goto10.org
Email: contact@goto10.org
Recent Projects: Pure:Dyne; Packet Forth; Make Art festival ... (works in progress)

1. What is your organisation's mission?

The mission of GOTO10 is to explore and support the fields of digital art, with a strong emphasis on open source software. We develop our own free software as well as trying to close the gap between the basic user and obscure developer nests. We focus on documentation by providing how to's and guides for various applications, and we are also now building a Linux based operating system dedicated to real time audio and video software in a user friendly environment. Another important point in GOTO10 is the regular production of live events such as workshops, concerts, installations and lectures.

3. Which communities do you support and how?

Initially, we tend to support ideas. Although ideally we offer services and support to communities where FLOSS is used as a basis for creativity, we also help other groups or individuals who belong to a different world. For us a production tool is a transitional object and the concept remains the most important element.

5. Do you see your work/labour as resisting, in symbiosis with, or exploited by capitalist production?

To be quite optimistic, I think we are neither resisting nor being exploited. These terms are marked with a very negative weight and some quite childish paranoia. To the contrary, I prefer to think we're in a phase of social and economic contamination. Our (FLOSS communities') ideas are ever more present in the media and everyone knows or has heard the term 'open source'. It is hard to imagine that platforms like Sourceforge were considered a futile playground for weirdos just a few years ago. Who would have imagined the overwhelming win on EU Patents? Who would have thought of Linux certification for desktop computers?

We are in a transitional phase and this is being achieved without revolution, wars or aggression which are the last breaths of a sick system. FLOSS is an intellectual virus, not a gun.

7. What licence, if any, do you use?

Any free licence that will fit any given project at any given time. We are not license fanatics or priests.

Your Name: Agnese Trocchi
Name of Organisation: New Global Vision (NGV)
Location: N/A
Website: http://www.ngvision.org/
Email: ngv@ecn.org

1. What is your organisation's mission?

To create an historical archive of independent videos. To organise a distribution network through peer-to-peer, FTP servers and RSS feeds. To establish a producers' and distributors' community which agrees on the use of Creative Commons licences and keeps track of its activities through ad hoc blogs. To develop a publishing, archiving, distribution set of software which is available for other communities to use. To be a useful tool for independent television stations which need to share and retrieve contents (see the Telestreets network: http://www.telestreet.it/)

2. What role does FLOSS play in your organisation's economy?

Without free software our project wouldn't exist at all. For two main reasons: the first is that free software allows us to build the technology to manage the archive and to make it available to users, from the website to the servers that host the archives. The second one is that only through free software have we been able to share and improve our knowledge and so be able to create the tools we need.

3. Which communities do you support and how?

We support the independent videomakers' community by giving it a tool to circulate its productions, and the independent TV commmunity by giving it a pool of materials to insert into its daily programmes.

5. Do you see your work/labour as resisting, in symbiosis with, or exploited by capitalist production?

Our work is not just resistant to capitalist production: it's creating new models of production. But as a community of independent videomakers we may say that (while waiting for the new world) we are still exploited by and in symbiosis with capitalist production.

6. What are the primary obstacles you face?

The lack of time that developers and editors can put into the work. We don't earn money from the project, and so we have to work on it in our spare time. Sometimes the most difficult thing is to meet face to face as these kinds of meetings are very important, but we are scattered all over Italy.

7. What licence, if any, do you use?

CC licences are applied to videos in the archive and we use the GPL for the set of softwares.

8. Do you see yourself as contributing to a commons?
Of course! NGV is one of the clearest examples of the creation of spaces for a commons, not only as regards licences, but also for the efforts that we put into accessibility, to content production and also for the will to develop a permanent archive.

Your Name: Chris
Name of Organisation: RampArt Hacklab.
Location: RampArt Social Centre, London
Website: http://wiki.hacklab.org.uk; http://www.rampart.co.nr
Email: guano@onetel.com
Recent Projects: RampArt Hacklab

1. What is your organisation's mission?
Spread the word about free/open source software, provide a resource for those wanting to actively work for a better society, have fun.

2. What role does FLOSS play in your organisation's economy?
The decision to use FLOSS was not at all based in economics. Most software is free (gratis) if you know where to look. The free (libre) aspect was all important.

3. Which communities do you support and how?
The loose global network of activists, individuals and groups engaged in social activism, by providing a computer resource for use and for skill sharing.

4. How do you participate within the production of code or how do you see your role within the FLOSS ecology?
I don't have any involvement with the production of code if I can persuade others to do it. I see my role as promoting FLOSS.

5. Do you see your work/labour as resisting, in symbiosis with, or exploited by capitalist production?
Definitely resisting by using and promoting alternatives to the products of capitalism.

6. What are the primary obstacles you face?
Propaganda/ mind share.

7. What licence, if any, do you use?
Operating system: BSD licence; X Window System: MIT X Window System licence; Other utilities: GPL and probably many others.

8. Do you see yourself as contributing to a commons?
Not directly as I don't create products but indirectly by promoting the products of the commons.

Your Name: Jaromil
Name of Organisation: Rastasoft
Location: Nomadic
Website: http://dyne.org, http://rastasoft.org, http://lab.dyne.org/Jaromil
Email: jaromil@dyne.org
Recent Projects: http://montevideo.dyne.org/trac.cgi/wiki/IvySync;
http://fakiir.dyne.org; http://freej.dyne.org; http://dynebolic.org;
http://muse.dyne.org

1. What is your organisation's mission?
This is Rasta software.

Jah Rastafari Livity bless our Freedom! This is free software, you should share it for the good of yourself and your people, respect others and let them express, be free and let others be free. Live long and prosper in Peace!

But remember there is no Peace without Justice. This software is about Resistance ina Babylon world which tries to control more and more the way we communicate and we share information and knowledge. This software is for all those who cannot afford to have the latest expensive hardware to speak out their words of consciousness and good will. This software has a full range of applications for the production and not only the fruition of information, it's a full multimedia studio and has no reason to envy other proprietary systems, because freedom and the sharing of knowledge are solid principles for evolution and that's where this software comes from.

Hic Sunt Leones. And much Blessings in Jah. Luv to All Those who still Resist. Selah.

2. What role does FLOSS play in your economy?
I have no business. I squat houses for a living. My economy is made out of solidarity. Thanks for yours.

3. Which communities do you support and how?
ASCII http://scii.nl, Indymedia and some others through writing code, recycling hardware, being a militant activist.

4. How do you participate within the production of code or how do you see your role within the FLOSS ecology?
I like Object Oriented and Multithreaded design. I code in C/C and Assembler. I like the way GNU/Linux, BSD and some other efforts are evolving, I've been contributing for more than 5 years and I do enjoy it a lot.

5. Do you see your work/labour as resisting, in symbiosis with, or exploited by capitalist production?
I don't know. I don't think anyone exploits me when using my software, I did it for a purpose and I'm happy to share it with people. I'm an anti-capitalist, which is not old fashioned since capitalism is still there, and I fight it, in many ways, including my code. Capitalism is about exploitation, in any case.

6. What are the primary obstacles you face?
Finding a house for living, finding food, finding peace to code.

7. What licence, if any, do you use?
GNU GPL for my code, Creative Commons for other things. In the early days I used Artistic Licence, Public Licence and Open Audio License from the EFF.

8. Do you see yourself as contributing to a commons?
Yes, indeed.

Your Name: Yves Degoyon
Name of Organisation: Riereta, Hackitectura, Indymedia Barcelona
Location: Barcelona
Website: http://www.riereta.net, http://www.hackitectura.net
Email: ydegoyon@free.fr
Recent Projects: Map-o-matix – collaborative environment for tactical cartography: http://mapomatix.sf.net; GISS/Gollum: streaming tools for social networks – http://gollum.artefacte.org; PiDiP – video extensions for Pure Data: http://ydegoyon.free.fr/pidip.html

1. What is your organisation's mission?
To develop accessible and open source software and build transnational networks for independent online medias, covering events from the World Social Forum 2005 to some hackmeeting in some anonymous place.

2. What role does FLOSS play in your organisation's economy?
All media and streams produced are made with open source software, and some specific tools http://mapomatix.sf.net are developed for our needs under the GPL.

3. Which communities do you support and how?
Indymedia, Plug'n'Politix, No One Is Illegal, Rotorrr http://www.rotorrr.org, V2V.

4. How do you participate within the production of code or how do you see your role within the FLOSS ecology?
We are free software dealers.

5. Do you see your work/labour as resisting, in symbiosis with, or exploited by capitalist production?
Our work is an alternative to the mainstream media (Al-jwarizmi versus CNN).

6. Why are the primary obstacles you face?
People wanting to rejoin the institutions. Academic writers disconnected from real people.

7. What licence, if any, do you use?
GPL.

8. Do you see yourself as contributing to a commons?
Ya, all our media content is free.

Your Name: Simon Yuill
Name of Organisation: N/A
Location: Glasgow
Website: http://www.spring-alpha.org
Email: simon@lipparosa.org
Recent Projects: http://www.spring-alpha.org; http://www.yourmachines.org

1. What is your mission?
I don't see myself in terms of 'missions' and such, I'm tactical rather than strategic if you like.

2. What role does FLOSS play in your economy?
Both creatively and financially it provides far greater possibilities – it foregrounds the cost of personal effort over packaged product (which is as it should be)

3. Which communities do you support and how?
No one group directly at present, but my work connects with various communities, principally other Glasgow based artists and local communities

4. How do you participate within the production of code or how do you see your role within the FLOSS ecology?
I write code. The *spring_alpha* project is not only implementing existing FLOSS (such as Soya 3D) but also providing a new style of 'live-coding' simulation tool which is available as a framework (under GPL) for others to use. I also encourage others to use or get involved with FLOSS through public workshops, talks, writing, (gentle) ranting and informal get togethers (we have a version of OpenLab in Glasgow which meets in people's flats).

5. Do you see your work/labour as resisting, in symbiosis with, or exploited by capitalist production?
Even if you choose the first option, resisting, under current conditions you are always implicated in the latter two. Dealing with this is the issue rather than simply claiming one status.

6. Why are the primary obstacles you face?
Getting up in the morning, but as I don't have a job this is not so bad.

7. What licence, if any, do you use?
GPL, Free Documentation Licence and versions of Creative Commons Licences depending on what's appropriate.

8. Do you see yourself as contributing to a commons?
Yes.

```
                              ,%%%,
                            % `%%%,
                           |' ) `%%,
                           \_/\  %%%,
                          _/      %%%--"""-.%,
                        /`_|                  \%
                        \\ \       /    |       /'
                        \]  | /----'.   <  `%
                                ||       `>> >
                                ||         ///`
                               /(          //(
```

PATENTLY OBVIOUS

The OpenMute project explains its approach to the public domain after four years of using and contributing to FLOSS

As a sister project of *Mute,* and in the context of *Mute*'s knowledge commons issue, OpenMute would like to clarify its position and relationship to FLOSS and the public domain. OpenMute involves different people from *Mute,* and the experiences, knowledge and day to day practices of those individuals bring a different and complimentary perspective to the issue of the 21st century commons.

The OpenMute project started in 2001 to provide FLOSS communications web tools to cultural and community groups, with an understanding of their shared circumstances: limited resources, mixed levels of computer skills, and often little experience of the networked communications that FLOSS facilitates. As an advocate of the public domain, OpenMute adopted FLOSS as a tactical media toolset for its ability to challenge the ongoing conversion of everyday knowledge into property. When shared conventions from daily life can be borrowed and patented just because they have been replicated in computer code, the office becomes the virtual office and CompuCorpX now own it. FLOSS and its associated strategies are a way of opposing these exploitative types of property and social relationships.

OpenMute's project now encompasses the following services: the free as in beer OM1 - a web CMS tool set now running over seven hundred individual web sites; the paid for OMXTRA; Web2POD print on demand, high quality low cost book production and distribution services; and recently, UserLand, a UK workshop tour with artists from across Europe advocating FLOSS cultural practice.

The public domain, which FLOSS is one method of contributing to, isn't a clear cut situation and is relatively new (as is the postNet world). OpenMute has taken the approach of being an active FLOSS user/participant/contributor, in order to help secure the public domain as a place of radical change and liberation alongside other groups. FLOSS is one component of what OpenMute terms the Free Technology Movement which also comprises; **Free networks** – community run and owned networks; **Free hardware standards** – non proprietary standards; **Peer2Peer networking** – such as Pirate Byran; **Open standards** – W3C; **Open content** – WikiPedia; **Open IP agreements** – Creative Commons.

Although many FLOSS practitioners might have stated their political agnosticism, it is this perceived neutrality that allows on the one hand the anti-

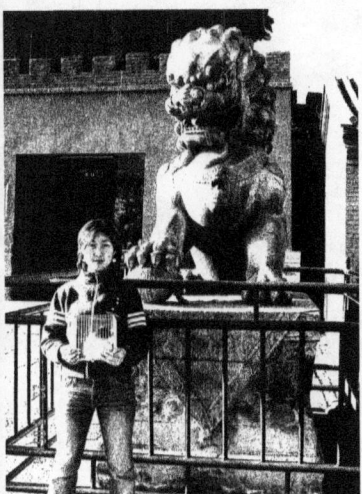

Image › OM user from Digital Media Studio - Bejing
http://dmsbeijing.omweb.org/

Capitalist movement to adopt FLOSS so readily and, on the other hand, corporations like IBM to see FLOSS as a more agile strategy for developing software and gaining ground on competitors like Microsoft.

OpenMute is funded by the Arts Council of England for its CMS web services OM1/OMXTRA and its UK FLOSS tour, UserLand. In a UK context OpenMute is in the same position as other FLOSS initiatives supported by the UK Government, whether it's in the area of education, the voluntary sector or community groups. The situation is one of accidental government involvement, with bottom up initiatives requesting support rather than the government having any policy or programmes which actively support FLOSS.

At a recent FLOSS voluntary groups event, SocialSource 2005, this situation was clearly underlined again and again as groups talked about their experiences. An example was Bristol Wireless which runs a scheme to provide primary school pupils with Linux installed laptops and a wireless connection to the school. The weak link is that the teachers are not trained in using Linux. Here a comparison can be made with Andalusia in the Iberian peninsular where there is an integrated FLOSS program by the government, and teachers are trained and supported in Linux. Another comparison is the ongoing support programme for the voluntary sector in the UK, called ChangeUp, where there is some FLOSS support. But again the initiative is piecemeal and only in its infancy, whereas in France local authorities run a local government SourceForge-like service, ADULLACT. If a government agency makes a FLOSS software package, for example to coordinate refuse collection, the software is put in a public repository for other government agencies to make use of.

Without integrated governmental support, initiatives face an uphill struggle. At last month's WSFII summit in London, which brought together players in the FTM, I overheard a conversion between two of the people attending, which sums up OpenMute's position on FLOSS: 'Why', a woman asked, 'are we having to build VOIP networks on a shoestring? Isn't this what the governments or the market should be up to?' And her friend replied, 'Yes, you would have thought so, but no they aren't, so it looks like it's DIY'. ⟋

URLS

OpenMute - http://openmute.org
SocialSource - http://www.socialsource.org.uk
ADULLACT – software mutualisation - http://www.adullact.org
Bristol Wireless - http://www.bristolwireless.net
WSFII World Summit of Free Information Infrastructures -
http://wsfii.org

Simon Worthington <simon@metamute.org> is the director of OpenMute and a lapsed artist

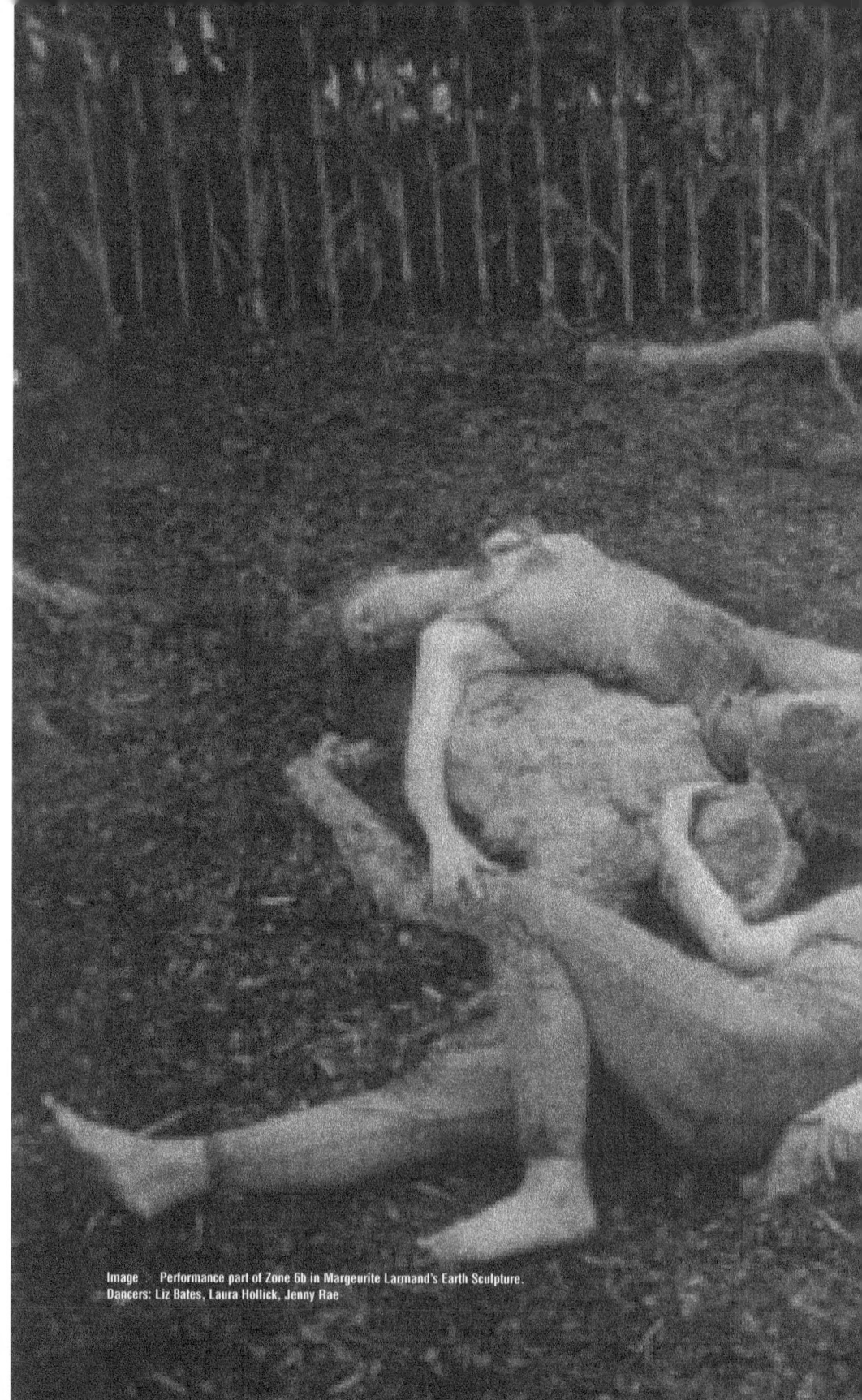

Image   Performance part of Zone 6b in Margeurite Larmand's Earth Sculpture.
Dancers: Liz Bates, Laura Hollick, Jenny Rae

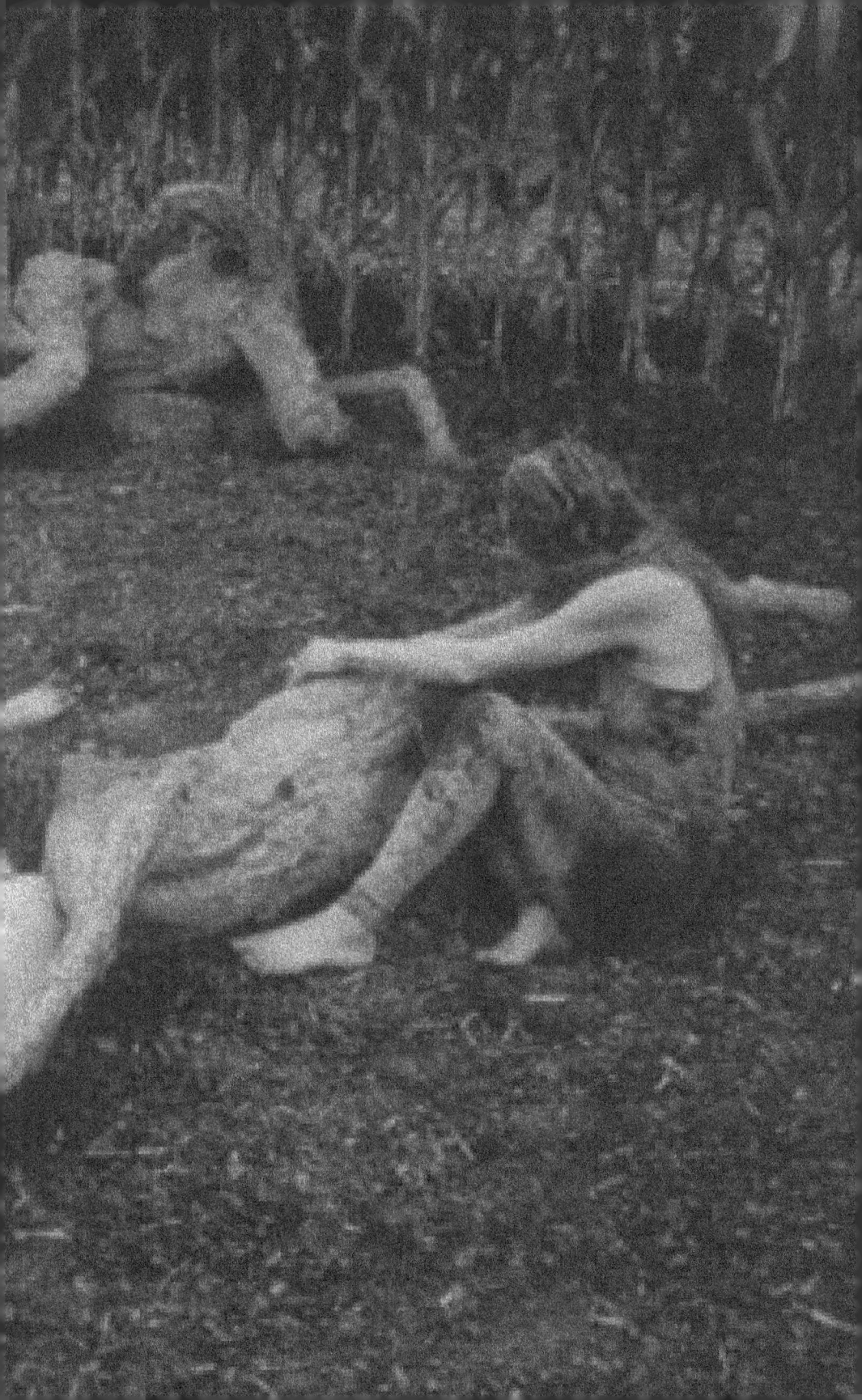

FLOSS REDUX: NOTES ON AFRICAN SOFTWARE POLITICS

The info-technological development of Africa is providing a critical laboratory for testing the utilitarian and egalitarian claims of the FLOSS community. The question of whether to adopt a free or proprietary route quickly expands beyond the immediate consideration of set up costs. Soenke Zehle considers how FLOSS fares in the competition to be the fittest 'tropical' technology, assesses different visions of continent-wide development, and examines FLOSS's own ambiguous economics

With a host of corporations, foundations, and organisations active in the fields of advocacy and assistance, free and open source software (FLOSS) has become a dynamic area of info-developmental cooperation. In the eminently pragmatic approach adopted by many of these efforts, the intense controversy over free vs. open source software and the extent to which advocacy should stress freedom over commercial applicability somehow seems a thing of the past. At the same time, the focus on FLOSS as an economic strategy of autonomous development within a global network capitalism rather than a post-capitalist practice of collaborative creation recalls some of the general ambivalences at the heart of software-political struggles.**1**

FOSSFA

In many African countries where computer users are not necessarily owners, important choices are often made by those in charge of establishing public ICT infrastructures. While many companies and organisations have chosen to adopt FLOSS on their own, the status of governments as the largest procurers of Information and

Communication Technology (ICT) means that government action is bound to stimulate industry in various ways, including the provision of FLOSS training and support. The recently founded Free Software and Open Source Foundation for Africa (FOSSFA), currently headquartered in Nairobi, Kenya, has therefore identified national ICT policy and procurement procedures as major advocacy targets.**2** For Bildad Kagai, co-founder and one of its secretaries, the licensing, localisation, and local skill building advantages of FLOSS, coupled with 'leapfrogging' technologies like wireless that help skip an entire generation of expensive infrastructural investments, offer an alternative to the technological dependency and resource drain associated with an exclusive reliance on mainstream proprietary software.

Given the many problems that beset the ICT sector in Africa, FLOSS advocacy is inevitably tied to political reforms in contracting, public services, and competition policy, as well as the creation of FLOSS related employment and business opportunities. Taking advantage of the organisational dynamic of WSIS and working closely with civil society organisations, corporations, and international donors, FOSSFA has created an effective advocacy coalition: Kenya's ICT policy now gives preference to open source (and open standards) over proprietary solutions, and FOSSFA also convinced the Committee on Development Information of the Economic Commission for Africa (CODI) to adopt a policy that prioritises FLOSS.

This is no small feat, given that many African states have yet to articulate any ICT policy whatsoever, and FOSSFA is also educating policy makers across the continent about FLOSS.**3** The 2004 Idlelo meeting in Capetown, co-organised by FOSSFA and the African Virtual Open Initiatives and Resources Project (AVOIR) at Western Cape University, was the 'First African Conference on the Digital Commons'.**4** Bringing some 200 FLOSS activists and developers from across the continent together with international researchers, Idlelo emphasised the need to shift from the mere adoption of FLOSS to the local development of FLOSS applications, the use of FLOSS in education, and the development of non-proprietary open content alternatives. Hoping to be able to recruit government representatives from all 53 African states, Idlelo 2 has already been scheduled for 2006.**5**

SOUTH AFRICA GOES OPEN SOURCE

The breakdown of Idlelo participants by country reveals the uneven geography of IT development in Africa: by far the largest contingent came from South Africa, followed by Nigeria and Kenya.**6** South Africa's influence in the African FLOSS movement is related to its dominance of the African IT sector at large. But there are other reasons, one of which is the impact of projects sponsored by Mark Shuttleworth.**7** Shuttleworth, a South African celebrity entrepreneur known for his space travel – Shuttleworth was the first 'afronaut' – as well as his philanthropic ambition, has overseen the development of Ubuntu (an already-popular Debian-and-GNOME based linux distribution updated in regular release cycles) and his Shuttleworth Foundation has co-launched a nation wide 'Go Open Source' campaign.**8**

Supported by the Meraka Intitute of the South African Council for Scientific and Industrial Research (CSIR) as well as HP and Canonical, the campaign has included the production of the first ever television series on open source – broadcast on public television and available for download – and the installation of 'Freedom Toasters', stand alone CD/DVD burners loaded with the latest FLOSS operating systems and applications, across South Africa.**9** In addition to working on an 'edubuntu' classroom version of its linux distribution, the Shuttleworth Foundation also works with South African schools to set up FLOSS-based thin client networks through its 'tuXlabs' initiative.**10** And following the 2005 'Go Open Source Task Team' conference, South Africa's national policy on free/open source software and open content is now being turned into an ambitious action plan.**11**

But is South Africa 'really' Africa? FOSSFA's Kagai notes that ICT developments in South Africa are not representative of Africa at large, and some see in the ideas of an 'African Renaissance' less a new Pan-Africanism than a mere culturalisation of South Africa's own economic and geopolitical ambition.**12** Yet it would be a mistake to associate less well off areas of the continent with a lack of interest in digital and network technologies – a point made years ago by none other than John Perry Barlow (ex-Grateful Dead and Electronic Frontier co-founder).**13** Barlow had concluded from his own experience of country life that Africans might have preserved a pre-industrial sense of connectedness and would want to bypass the crippling effects of an individualist industrialism to embrace the digital technologies of the network society. Even after the dotcom crash, his occasionally, albeit ironically, exoticist travelogue is still worth a read, in part because much of his 'let's wire Africa' enthusiasm was shared by the initial wave of international ICT task forces that were to turn the new economy experience into a fully fledged paradigm of info-development. And it encouraged Russell Southwood, a former UK management consultant, to start Balancing Act Africa, already one of the most important information services on ICT related developments across Africa, including the failures and successes of FLOSS advocacy.**14**

Perhaps somewhat surprisingly, FLOSS has not been an easy sell. One reason, suggests Ethan Zukerman, might be the overemphasis on free beer at the expense of free speech; a reference to Richard Stallmann's famous definition of free software.**15** Zukerman, a co-founder of GeekCorps – 'an international non-profit organisation that transfers tech skills from geeks in developed nations to geeks in emerging nations' – and initiator of 'BlogAfrica', believes that many African users continue to associate 'inexpensive' with 'inferior', a legacy of technology transfer and appropriate technology projects that sometimes amounted to little more than the dumping of obsolete technology.**16** And in areas where non-licensed copies of proprietary software are widely available as well as a great deal of corresponding 'street' expertise, comparatively expensive manuals and a lack of bandwidth for accessing online support can easily increase the total cost of ownership of non-proprietary alternatives generally assumed to be 'free'. FLOSS advocates should stress the expandability, transparency and resulting high performance of their software instead.

While a growing number of studies make an empirically based case for FLOSS in general, less is known about the experiences of FLOSS adoption across Africa.**17** One such report has been published by Bridges.org, an international NGO with offices in South Africa and the US.**18** According to Bridges.org, the availability of the source code is an advantage actually rarely exploited at the computer lab level, whereas the cost of software licenses – the 'free beer' argument – remains a key concern, especially evident when these costs are expressed in terms of GDP share. Among the factors that lower software costs, piracy is the most important, followed by donations and so called thin-client configurations that bring back to life hardware generally considered obsolete. FLOSS, concludes the report, has become a mainstream alternative. Yet because of the level of expertise required to establish and maintain a FLOSS based computer lab, it tends to work better in large projects that have the resources to address the practical problems of migration, training, and support, in contrast to individual labs that can simply take advantage of proprietary solutions that are already in place.

INFO-POLITICAL VISIONS

Beyond the issue of appropriate means, how do the local politics of software relate to competing visions of what 'info-development' is and should be about? In the larger info-political vision that frames local decisions over software and standards, questions of autonomy are central, frequently articulated in response to the hegemonic presence of corporate software and IT giants. FLOSS advocates have criticised the most recent wave of international public private partnerships in this area, for example, because they involve only the usual transnational suspects. Microsoft, HP, and Cisco are all well represented in the activities of major development agencies, advertising themselves as 'partners in development' to promote ICTs as the vehicles for 'good governance' and 'effective service delivery', but also to stake out their own commercial claims, crowd out grassroots or public sector alternatives, and subvert South-South cooperation.

Take SchoolNet Namibia.**19** Having to work with substantially fewer resources than the Shuttleworth Foundation, SchoolNet has

Where pirated software is widely available, comparatively expensive manuals and lack of access to online support can increase the real cost of 'free' alternatives

'Most of the so-called "technology transfers" are essentially excuses for transnational corporations to take over local companies, or to carve out a share of the domestic markets'

nevertheless set up FLOSS-based thin client networks in over a hundred schools, launched an ISP to offer subsidised internet service, and is exploring the set up of wireless access in rural areas. Once they had found that students were a lot more likely to embrace FLOSS than their teachers, and standard advocacy tools were not doing much to change that, SchoolNet launched Hai Ti ('Listen Up!'), a comic strip that features real life FLOSS users.**20** Its contractual agreement with schools specifies that the teams who manage the local computer lab include students as well as teachers. Yet occasionally, SchoolNet finds that their FLOSS-LANs remain unmaintained while students use equipment donated by Microsoft and administered with support from MS certified engineers. Executive director Joris Komen is convinced that Microsoft has targeted Namibian schools specifically because SchoolNet Namibia has become an outspoken critic of the company and its philosophy.**21**

Commenting on recent agreements between Microsoft and the New Partnership for African Development (NEPAD), the United Nations Development Programme (UNDP), and the United Nations High Commissioner for Refugees (UNHCR), Bildad Kaigai of FOSSFA agrees that such deals work to confine the software choices these agencies can make and effectively transfer wealth away from an emergent local software industry. Kagai calls on African leaders to emulate the successful development strategies of Asian countries instead.**22**

Other ICT analysts note, however, that African countries will have to do so under dramatically different circumstances. Yash Tandon of SEATINI stresses that 'most of the so-called "technology transfers" ... are essentially excuses for transnational corporations (TNCs) to take over local companies, or to carve out a share of the domestic markets.'**23** Rather than 'stripping naked' to attract foreign direct investment (FDI) from the North, Tandon also makes the case for the 'creation of a home based Domestic Scientific and Technology Capacity (DSTC), including capacity to undertake relevant research and development, the actual purchase (as opposed to transfer) of appropriate technology from the open market, and a transfer of technology, preferably between South-South, only under certain conditions.' But Tandon also notes that options exploited by the 'Asian Tigers' are no longer available to Africa: 'Countries such as Korea and Taiwan, as all other now advanced economies in history, were able to do it because they disembedded the technology from its capital base (by, for example, copying intellectual property, and through reverse engineering), and by creating a 'national' base for capital. Some countries were able to do this during the cold war years when the West needed them to fight against the

Communist threat coming from China and Vietnam. ... Since the end of the cold war, this option is no longer available. ... Now, with intellectual property rights embedded in the World Trade Organisation (WTO) under the Trade Related Aspects of Intellectual Property Rights (TRIPS), scientific knowledge has become monopolised in the hands of a few thousand multinational corporations that use this knowledge to control the economies of the third world.' For Tandon, Africa has only so many options: 'It is in this context that Africa must develop its own DSTC, including a policy on relevant research and development. The R&D policy must be based on the production conditions in the region, the need first to produce for the domestic/regional market (only secondarily for the export market), and Africa's location within the global value chain.'

It seems that third worldist strategies sustained by a generalised critique of neocolonialism have been replaced by the exhausting creation of advocacy networks that hold local governments just as accountable as transnational corporations.**24** Yet while visions of Africa's future have sobered significantly, the emergent dynamic of South-South cooperation still echoes a tricontinentalist spirit. Brazil's official commitment to what its minister of culture, Gilberto Gil, has refererred to as a 'tropicalisation' of open source has been a major push for FLOSS advocacy in Africa. One such example of a South-South technology transfer was Brazil's support for the adoption and implementation of open source software for the management of Top Level Domain (TLD) registries in a number of African countries, a process that will eventually automate TLD registries.**25**

An increasing 'post-third worldist' cooperation is visible in other international info-political fora as well. One example is the campaign for a 'WIPO Development Agenda' and a Treaty for Access to Knowledge, supported by a broad coalition of southern governments as well as grassroots organisations.**26** The World Intellectual Property Organisation is a UN agency whose current mandate is 'the maintenance and further development of the respect for intellectual property throughout the world.' In the eyes of its critics, this mandate limits WIPO to the role of an enforcer of Euro-American positions on intellectual property, supporting the WTO's Agreement on Trade Related Aspects of Intellectual Property Rights (TRIPS) as well as at least condoning the aggressive 'TRIPS-Plus' bilateralism both the US and the EU have engaged in to effectively bypass the ongoing review process of key TRIPS provisions.**27** The access-to-knowledge campaign puts the question of FLOSS and the struggle over open standards in a much broader context. WIPO defines creativity in relation to the prospect of proprietisation, as culture is defined as the creation of private property. The FLOSS controversy, on the other hand, is not just about reducing the cost of running a computer lab, but over the implications of its approach to 'commons-based peer production' (Yochai Benkler): i.e. processes of collaborative creation and an information and knowledge commons actively enlarged in opposition to the 'second enclosure' (James Boyle) associated with an ever expanding IPR regime.**28**

Soft's software is based on 'tropically relevant' code: frequent savings to disk help deal with power failures, work offline lowers costs for internet access, storage on remote servers avoids interruptions caused by changes of government

Take the role of FLOSS developers. Rishab Ghosh, FLOSS Program Leader at the Maastricht Economic Research Institute on Innovation and Technology (MERIT), stresses that licensing costs do matter, especially when GDP is taken into account.**29** But another key emphasis in his studies on FLOSS in developing countries is on the skills-building in FLOSS networks. In addition to standard developer skills, open source communities address, almost by default, questions of copyright law and licensing, and introduce users to new forms of collaborative creation. Ghosh calls these 'informal apprenticeships' whose social cost is, of course, borne by individual users, but it is done so voluntarily, and he even considers the free sharing of developer expertise (often based on expensive degrees) a form of technology transfer. Most definitely exploited by employers who often encourage their employees to participate in FLOSS fora on the job, this voluntarist dynamic is also the basis of networks of 'roving technology consultants' like GeekCorps or E-Riders, as well as the collaborative practices of the FLOSS community at large.**30**

INFO-POLITICAL PRAGMATISM

Ghosh has been a major global FLOSS advocate, and his projects specifically address the use of FLOSS outside Europe. Yet some of his economic arguments are based on the assumption that proprietary alternatives are not locally produced. What Ghosh describes as the benefits of 'deep access' offered by locally developed FLOSS applications – customisation, quick bug fixing, as well as the re-use of code in other applications – is exactly how Herman Chinery-Hesse, CEO of Ghana's successful Soft Tribe, describes his own approach.**31** All of Soft's software is based on 'tropically relevant' code, Chinery-Hesse's reference to the full spectrum of constraints he associates with local computer use: frequent savings to disk help deal with power failures and work offline lowers costs for online access. In the case of Soft's document management software for the Ghana Human Rights Commission, storage on remote servers addresses possible interruptions caused by a change in government. And unlike Ubuntu, Soft's applications are optimised for the low-end hardware that dominates Ghana's offices and cybercafés.

Soft trains the majority of Ghana's programmers, often left to their own devices in poorly equipped computer science departments. Yet Chinery-Hesse thinks that FLOSS would impede the development of a local software industry, as developers would, he worries, be reduced to installers of pre-existing applications. His main concern, however, seems to be possible tampering with the code both by users and competitors – Chinery-Hesse fears internal mismanagement and has no interest in interoperability that could threaten Soft's pole position in the local software market. Soft rarely releases beta versions, software does not have an autoinstall function, and bug fixes are not generally released. Evidence of Chinery-Hesse's entrepreurial pragmatism, he has also entered into a cooperation agreement with Microsoft, hoping to take advantage of its global distribution channels to bring an add on from Ghana to desktops around the world.

For Guido Sohne, a former Soft employee and vocal FLOSS advocate, Soft's deal with Microsoft is a form of technology transfer rather than a simple sell-out, prompted by the departure of some of its key developers without whom their previous portfolio of applications could no longer be maintained.**32** Sohne left in part because Soft did not want to explore FLOSS-based alternatives to address this development impasse. Microsoft is there to stay (the new Kofi Annan International Peacekeeping Centre in Ghana also entered into a deal with Microsoft), but it looks like Soft's emergent competitors are already relying on FLOSS. So while Ghana's developer community as a whole has not yet embraced FLOSS, this is likely to change.

In the current 'Africanisation' of the politics of software, the proprietary/non-proprietary divide is but one of several vectors. Perhaps this should not come as a surprise, given the hybrid dynamic of FLOSS itself. In her analyses of the cooperation between corporations and the FLOSS community, techno-feminist Yuwei Lin describes this process as 'hybrid innovation', marked as much by a sense of interdependence and mutuality as by unease over the irresolvable tension between commercial and community-oriented practices.**33**

The dependence on corporate support illustrates the paradoxes of immaterial labour and suggests that common assumptions regarding the relationship between FLOSS and visions of a post-capitalist future be revisited. Often understood in terms of an anti-monopolistic practice, FLOSS is not, as such, anti-capitalist (GPL-founder Richard Stallman describes himself as anti-fascist instead). One of the reasons for the popularity of the FLOSS paradigm is that it appears to be able to accommodate a wide range of visions of cultural, economic, and social transformation, from cyberlibertarian views of natural capitalism to the post-autonomist vision of a coming communism, actively anticipated by way of multitudinal self-organisation. Countercultural cachet notwithstanding, the high visibility of FLOSS as a mainstream alternative to proprietary software is due in large part to the support from corporations like IBM or Sun Microsystems, and the commitment to

dependence on corporate support suggests that common assumptions regarding the relationship between FLOSS and visions of a post-capitalist future be revisited

openness reverberates with an info-capitalism attempting to reinvent itself around concepts of trust and transparency.

And while the controversies over software licenses are so intense because their clauses redefine what property means in the network society, not all of FLOSS is geared toward an enlargement of the information commons. Following the popularity of user-defined license provisions like Creative Commons, Sun Microsystems has announced its own 'Open Media Commons' initiative to develop FLOSS based digital rights management tools.**34** FLOSS, already adopted by cost cutting governments across the world, is also easily aligned with state power – South Africa's FLOSS and open content strategy includes, after all, the migration to FLOSS of its prison management systems.**35** This makes one-size-fits-all approaches to the politics of software almost impossible, even more so in the context of African ICT controversies.

Yet what is certain is that an African info-politics is already emerging along key faultlines of network-economical conflict, challenging images of an Africa forever mired in 'tribal rampages' and natural disasters. And while it is too soon to say what transformative impact FLOSS efforts may already have had, examples like FOSSFA or SchoolNet show that FLOSS is not reducible to an imperial voluntarism out of sync with the 'real' Africa. FLOSS's collaborative ethic is not a post-materialist luxury limited to those on the sunny side of the digital divide. Instead, the Africanisation of FLOSS in terms of an 'ubuntu' philosophy of sharing may soon connect to other collective efforts in a larger Pan-African vision of renewal. This project driven mainly from below is rarely included in the sovereign perspective of afro-pessimist prophecies accompanying the current wave of imperial nostalgia.**36** In his documentary *afro@digital*, Congolese director Balufu Bakupa-Kanyinda retrieves the story of the Ishango Bone, the oldest known table of prime numbers, to suggest that mathematics, and by implication the network society as a whole, needs to be given a new, Afrocentric genealogy. FLOSS advocacy may not have to go that far. Yet perhaps a discussion of software politics in Africa should not begin with the question of software, but with the contradictory images of Africa that linger in the collective post-colonial imagination.   ⌇

FOOTNOTES

----

1 For an account of free software vs open source software in terms of a struggle over discursive hegemony, see David Berry, 'The Contestation of Code: A preliminary investigation into the discourse of the free/libre and open source movements', *Critical Discourse Studies* 1.1 (April 2004), 65–89, http://opensource.mit.edu/papers/berry1.pdf

2 http://FOSSFA.net

3 Bildad Kagai and Nicolas Kimolo, 'FOSSFA in Africa: Opening the Door to State ICT Development Agendas – A Kenya Case Study', SSRC The Politics of Open Source Adoption (2005), http://www.ssrc.org/wiki/POSA; CODI, 'Resolutions of the Fourth Meeting of the Committee on Development Information (CODI-IV)', UNECA Commission on Development Information (23-28 April 2005), http://www.uneca.org/codi/codi4/codi_iv_report.pdf. See the country policy tables at: http://www.bridges.org/FLOSS/index.html

4 http://avoir.uwc.ac.za/

5 www.FOSSFA.net/idlelo2

6 Derek Keats, 'Idlelo: First African Conference on the Digital Commons', Final Report to Department of Science & Technology South Africa (2004), http://www.catia.ws/Documents/Indexpage/IdleloFinalReport.pdf

7 http://www.markshuttleworth.com

8 http://www.ubuntulinux.org, http://www.go-opensource.org/

9 http://www.freedomtoaster.org/, http://www.go-opensource.org/go_open

10 http://www.edubuntu.org/, http://www.tuxlab.org.za/;. A thin client is a computer (client) in client-server architecture networks which have very few resources, so it has to depend primarily on the central server for processing activities. A thin client network centralises maintenance tasks on a (remote) server

11 http://wiki.go-opensource.org/taskforce

12 For a middle of the road assessment of the African Renaissance, see Elias K. Bongmba, 'Reflections on Thabo Mbeki's African Renaissance', *Journal of Southern African Studies* 30.2 (June 2004). For more critical views, see Neil Lazarus, 'The South African Ideology: The Myth of Exceptionalism, the Idea of Renaissance,' *South Atlantic Quarterly* 103.4 (Fall 2004), 607-28, and Neville Alexander, 'South Africa – Example or Illusion?' *An Ordinary Country: Issues in the Transition from Apartheid to Democracy in South Africa*, New York: Berghahn Books, 2003, 137-73, 188-90

13 John Perry Barlow, 'Africa Rising', *Wired* 6.01 (1998) http://www.wired.com/wired/archive/6.01/barlow_pr.html

14 http://www.balancingact-africa.com/

15 Ethan Zukerman, 'Free Beer Doesn't Sell', *Linux Journal* 111 (July 2003) http://www.linuxjournal.com/article/6785

16 http://www.geekcorps.org/, http://www.ethanzuckerman.com/blog/

17 David Wheeler, 'Why Open Source Software / Free Software (OSS/FS, FLOSS, or FLOSS)? Look at the Numbers!', (May 2005) http://www.dwheeler.com/oss_fs_why.html

18 Bridges.org, 'Comparison study of Free/Open Source and Proprietary Software in an African context: implementation and policy-making to optimise community access to ICT' (May 2005) http://www.bridges.org/software_comparison/index.html

19 http://www.schoolnet.na/

20 http://www.schoolnet.na/haiti

21 http://tatejoris.blogspot.com

22 Bildad Kagai, 'FOSSFA responds to Microsoft-UNDP Deal' (Feb 2004), http://FOSSFA.net

23 Yash Tandon, 'An Alternative View on Technology', SEATINI (Sept 2004), http://www.seatini.org/publications/factsheets/technology.htm

24 Thandika Mkandawire, 'Good Governance: The Itinerary of an Idea', *D + C Development and Cooperation* 31.10 (01 Oct 2004) http://www.inwent.org/E+Z/content/archive-eng/10-2004/tribune_art1.html

25 Rebecca Wanjiku, 'Brazil opens its arms to Africa', *Highway Africa News Agency* (05 April 2005) http://www.highwayafrica.ru.ac.za/hana/textviewer.asp?item_id=339

26 http://www.cptech.org/a2k/, http://www.eff.org/IP/WIPO/dev_agenda/,

http://www.access2knowledge.org/cs/

27 Peter Drahos and John Brathwaite, 'Who Owns the Knowledge Economy? Political Organising Behind TRIPS', *Corner House Briefings* 32 (Sept 2004), http://www.thecorner-house.org.uk/pdf/briefing/32trips.pdf, also see http://www.bilaterals.org/

28 Yochai Benkler, 'Coase's Penguin, or Linux and the Nature of the Firm' (2002) http://www.benkler.org/CoasesPenguin.html; James Boyle, 'A Politics of Intellectual Property: Environmentalism For the Net?' (1997) http://www.law.duke.edu/boylesite/intprop.htm

29 Rishab Ghosh, 'Free/Libre/Open Source Software for developing countries: skills, employment and costs', 2nd National Congress on Software Libre, Buenos Aires, Argentina (07 June 2005), http://www.flossproject.org/papers.htm

30 http://www.eriders.net

31 G. Pascal Zachary, 'The African Hacker,' *IEEE Spectrum Online* (Aug 2005), http://www.spectrum.ieee.org/WEBONLY/publicfeature/aug05/0805ahac.html

32 My assessment of Soft is based on an email exchange with Guido Sohne (Sept 2005). Also see http://sohne.net.

33 Yuwei Lin, 'Hybrid Innovation: How Does the Collaboration Between the FLOSS Community and Corporations Happen?' *Knowledge, Technology and Policy* 18.2 (Summer 2005), http://opensource.mit.edu/papers/lin4_hybrid.pdf

34 http://www.openmediacommons.org/. As the history of commons-based resource management systems shows, 'commons' doesn't necessarily imply the free-for-all often associated with it, and it is not necessarily obvious – a point made frequently by advocates of indigenous and traditional knowledge databases, for example – that 'commons' and 'access restrictions' are mutually exclusive; what emerges instead are 'hybridised' commons that take the information needs of specific communities into account.

35 http://wiki.go-opensource.org/taskforce/CorrectProj

36 Martin Meredith, *The State of Africa: A History of Fifty Years of Independence*, London: Free Press, 2005; Seumas

Milne, 'Britain: imperial nostalgia', *Le Monde Diplomatique* (May 2005). Also see Chris Landsberg and Shaun Mckay, 'Engaging the new Pan-Africanism', Centre for Policy Studies (Sept 2005) http://www.sarpn.org.za/documents/d0001537/CSO-Guide_pan-africanism_2005.pdf

Soenke Zehle <s.zehle@kein.org> teaches transcultural media studies at Saarland University, Germany

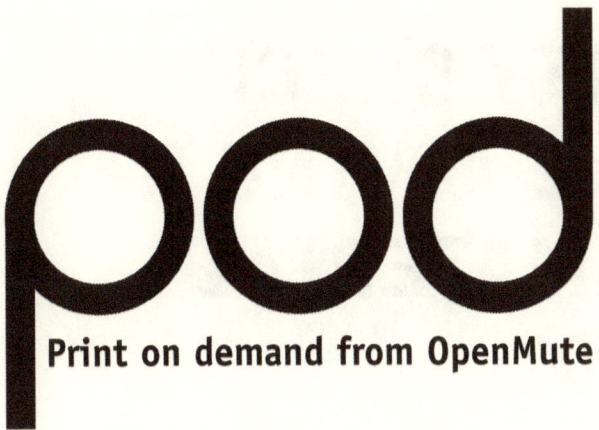

Print on demand from OpenMute

OpenMute POD allows you to print books in numbers from 1 to 100+ at a fixed price of just £1.34 per book. Instead of having to fork out a lot of money at the start of your book project you just pay as you print.

POD is a professional digital printing method that offers high quality black and white print bound with colour covers. POD has existed in the corporate sector, at a high price, but only now with new web services has it become accessible and affordable to the public. In combination with the web, POD takes all the headache out of print setup and delivery to the printers. It makes sales and distribution simpler, too.

Drawing on our expertise in web and print publishing, OpenMute offers a full range of services at budget prices to help you make your POD book. In the spirit of knowledge sharing we have a complete 'how to' available free online if you want to learn about the process and make your own DIY PODs.

OpenMute services include:

* Document preparation and delivery to the POD printer
* Customer online ordering and delivery service
* Integration into an existing web site
* Consultancy and training

If you'd like to talk more or get a free quote for your POD, then please get in touch: <services@metamute.org>

OpenMute POD info, http://openmute.org/news/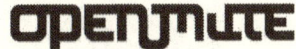

REALITY CHECK: ARE WE LIVING IN AN IMMATERIAL WORLD?

Immaterial Labour is seen by (post)Marxists and capitalists alike as the motor of the new economy. Steve Wright recovers Marx's theory of value from critics such as Antonio Negri to ask whether it is as 'immeasurably' productive as is claimed?

> *A priest once came across a Zen master and, seeking to embarrass him, challenged him as follows: 'Using neither sound nor silence, can you show me what is reality?'*
> *The Zen master punched him in the face.*[1]

Continued assertions that, today, we live in a knowledge economy or society raise many questions for reflection. In the next few pages, I want to discuss some aspects of these assertions, especially as they relate to the notion of immaterial labour. This term has developed within the camp of thought that is commonly labelled 'postworkerist', of which the best known exponent is undoubtedly Antonio Negri. While its roots lie in that branch of postwar Italian Marxism known as *operaismo* (workerism), this milieu has rethought and reworked many of the precepts developed during the Italian New Left's heyday of 1968-78. If anything, it was the very defeat of the social subjects with which *operaismo* had identified – first and foremost, the so-called 'mass worker' engaged in the production of consumer durables through repetitive, 'semi-skilled labour' – that led Negri and others to insist that we are embarked upon a new age beyond modernity.[2]

According to this view of the world, a quite different kind of labour is currently either hegemonic amongst those with nothing to sell but their ability to work – or, at the very least, is well on the way towards acquiring such hegemony. Secondly, capital's growing dependence upon this different – *immaterial* – labour has serious implications for the process of self-expanding abstract labour (value) that defines capital as a social relation. While Marx had held that the 'socially-necessary labour-time' associated with their production provided the means by which capital could measure the value of commodities (and so the mass of surplus value that it hoped to realise with their sale), Negri, on the other hand, is of the opinion that in a time of increasingly complex and skilled labour, and of a working day that more and more blurs the boundaries with (and ultimately colonises) the rest of our waking hours, value can no longer be calculated. As he put it a decade ago, in such circumstances the exploitation of labour still continues, but 'outside any economic measure: its economic reality is fixed exclusively in political terms.'**3**

This is pretty esoteric stuff, particularly the arguments over the measurability (or otherwise) of value. Should we care one way or the other? What I hope to show below is that for all their apparent obscurity, these debates matter. That is because they raise questions as to how we understand our immediate context, including how we interpret the possibilities latent within contemporary class composition. Is one sector of class composition likely to set the pace and tone in struggles against capital, or should we look instead towards the emergence of 'strange loops ... odd circuits and strange connections between and among various class sectors' (as Midnight Notes once suggested) as a necessary condition for moving beyond 'the present state of things'?

UNPACKING IMMATERIAL LABOUR

Maurizio Lazzarato's discussion of 'Immaterial Labour' was perhaps the first extended treatment of the topic to appear in English. Part of an important anthology of Italian texts published in the mid '90s, Lazzarato's work defined the term immaterial labour as 'labour that produces the informational and cultural content of the commodity.'**4** If the 'classic' forms of this labour were represented in fields like 'audiovisual production, advertising, fashion, the production of software, photography, cultural activities, and so forth', those who perform such work commonly found themselves in highly casualised, precarious and exploited circumstances, as part of what, more recently and in certain Western European radical circles, has come to be called the 'precariat'.**5**

The Taylorist approach to production that confronted the mass worker had decreed that 'you are not paid to think'. With immaterial labour, Lazzarato argued, management's project was different. In fact, it was even more totalitarian than the earlier rigid division between mental and manual labour (ideas and execution), because capitalism seeks to involve even the worker's personality within the production of value.**6**

At the same time this managerial approach carried real risks for capital, Lazzarato believed, since capital's very existence was placed in the hands of a labour force called upon to exercise its creativity through collective endeavours. And unlike a century ago, when a layer of skilled workers likewise stood at the centre of key industries, yet largely cut off from the unorganised 'masses', today 'immaterial labour' could not be understood as the distinctive attribute of one stratum within the workforce. Instead, skilled labour is present (even if only in latent form) amongst broad sectors of the labour market, starting with the young.

Michael Hardt and Antonio Negri's *Empire* – a book that has come to stand (rightly or wrongly) as the centrepiece of postworkerist thought – built upon and modified Lazzarato's work. Accepting the premise that immaterial labour was now central to capital's survival (and by extension, to projects that aimed at its extinction), Hardt and Negri identified three segments of immaterial labour:

> a) the reshaped instances of industrial production which had embraced communication as their lifeblood;
> b) the 'symbolic analysis and problem solving' undertaken by knowledge workers;
> c) the affective labour found above all within the service sector.**7**

These experiences, it was conceded, could be quite disparate: knowledge workers, for example, were divided between high-end practitioners with considerable control over their working conditions, while others engaged in 'low-value and low-skill jobs of routine symbol manipulation'.**8** Nonetheless a common thread did exist between the three elements. As instances of service work, none of them produced a 'material or durable good'. Moreover, since the output was physically intangible as a discrete object, so the labour that produced it could be designated as 'immaterial'.**9**

How can we make sense of such arguments? Doug Henwood, who praised *Empire* for the verve and optimism of its vision, was nonetheless moved to add:

> Hardt and Negri are often uncritical and credulous in the face of orthodox propaganda about globalization and immateriality ... They assert that immaterial labour – service work, basically – now prevails over the old-fashioned material kind, but they don't cite any statistics: you'd never expect that far more Americans are truck drivers than are computer professionals. Nor would you have much of an inkling that three billion of us, half the earth's population, live in the rural Third World, where the major occupation remains tilling the soil.**10**

Nick Dyer-Witheford has likewise registered a number of concerns with Hardt and Negri's account of class composition.**11** To his mind, *Empire* glosses over the tensions between the three class fragments it identifies, while ultimately reading immaterial labour only through the lenses of its high-end manifestations. And was all of this really as new as Hardt and Negri intimated? It's not as if 'affective labour', for instance, was anything but fundamental to social reproduction in the past, even if it did go unnoticed – because of its largely gendered composition perhaps – in many social analyses.

Another issue concerns *Empire*'s insistence that 'the cooperative aspect of immaterial labour is not imposed or organised from the outside'.**12** Again, perhaps this is true for some work at the high-end. But does the obligation to ask 'Do you want fries with that?' really represent a break with Fordist work regimes? Or might many of the McJobs that are prevalent in the lower depths of so-called immaterial production be better characterised as 'the Taylorised, deskilled descendants of earlier forms of office' and other service work?**13**

More recently, Hardt and Negri have attempted to address some of their critics in *Multitude*, the 2004 sequel to *Empire*. The first thing to note here is that while immaterial labour remains a central pivot within the book's arguments, it is presented in a rather more cautious and qualified form than before. Indeed, Hardt and Negri are at pains to state that:

a) 'When we claim that immaterial labour is tending towards the hegemonic position we are not saying that most of the workers in the world today are producing primarily immaterial goods';

b) 'The labour involved in all immaterial production, we should emphasise, remains material – it involves our bodies and brains as all labour does. What is immaterial is *its product*.'**14**

Therefore, much like the ascendance of the multitude itself, here the hegemony of immaterial labour as the reference point, or even vanguard, for 'most of the workers in the world today' is flagged as a tendency, albeit one that is inexorable. Towards the end of *Multitude*'s discussion of immaterial labour, Hardt and Negri insist upon what they call a 'reality check' – 'what evidence do we have to substantiate our claim of a hegemony of immaterial labour?'**15** It's the moment we've all been waiting for, and unfortunately the half a page of discussion they proffer is something of a damp squib: an allusion to US Bureau of Statistics figures which indicate that service work is on the

three billion of us, half the earth's population, live in the rural Third World, where the major occupation remains tilling the soil

does the obligation to ask 'do you want fries with that?' really represent a break with Fordist work regimes?

rise; the relocation of industrial production 'to subordinate parts of the world', said to signal the privileging of immaterial production at the heart of the Empire; the rising importance of 'immaterial forms of property'; and, finally, the spread of network forms of organisation particular to immaterial labour.**16** Call me old-fashioned, but something more than this is needed in a book of 400 plus pages dedicated to understanding their claims regarding latest manifestation of the proletariat as a revolutionary subject...

Their reference to the growth in service sector activity is interesting for a number of reasons. Huws argues that the unrelenting rise in service work within the West might be cast in a different light if the domestic employment so common 100 years ago was factored into the equation.**17** Writing a decade earlier, Sergio Bologna suggested that certain forms of work only came to be designated as 'services' within national statistics *after* they had been outsourced; previously, when they had been performed 'in house', they had counted as 'manufacturing'.**18** Neither author is seeking to deny that important shifts have occurred within the global economy, starting with countries like Britain, Australia, Canada and the United States. Yet they urge caution in how we interpret the changes, and care in the categories used to explain them. Bologna – a one-time collaborator with Negri in a variety of political projects back in the '60s and '70s – is particularly caustic about the notion of immaterial labour, labelling it a 'myth' that more than anything else obscures the lengthening of the working day.**19**

GOODBYE TO VALUE AS MEASURE?

As stated earlier, one of the distinguishing features of postworkerism is the rejection of Marx's so-called 'law of value'. George Caffentzis reminds us that Marx himself rarely spoke of such a law, but there is also no doubt of his opinion that, under the rule of capital, the amount of labour time socially necessary to produce commodities ultimately determined their value.**20** In breaking with Marx in this regard, postworkerists draw some of their inspiration instead from a passage in the *Grundrisse* known as the 'Fragment on Machines'. This envisages a situation, in line with capital's perennial attempt to free itself from dependence upon labour, where knowledge has become the lifeblood of fixed capital, and the direct input of labour to production is merely incidental. In these circumstances, Marx argues, capital effectively cuts the ground from under its own feet, for 'As soon as labour in the direct form has ceased to be the great well-spring of wealth, labour time ceases and must cease to be its measure, and hence exchange value [must cease to be the measure] of use value'.**21**

Negri, among others, has insisted for many years, and in a variety of ways, that capital has now reached this stage. Therefore, nothing but sheer domination keeps its

capital is always obliged to pose 'labour time as sole measure and source of wealth'

rule in place: 'the logic of capital is no longer functional to development, but is simply command for its own reproduction'.**22** In fact a range of social commentators have evoked the 'Fragment on Machines' in recent times – apart from anything else, it has held a certain popularity amongst those (like reactionary futurologist Jeremy Rifkin) who tell us that we live in an increasingly work-free society. It's a pity, then, that few of these writers follow the logic of Marx's argument in the *Grundrisse* to its conclusions. For while he indicates that capital does indeed seek 'to reduce labour time to a minimum', Marx also reminds us that capital is itself nothing other than accumulated labour time (abstract labour as value).**23** In other words, capital is obliged by its very nature, and for as long as we are stuck with it, to pose 'labour time ... as sole measure and source of wealth.'

In its efforts to escape from labour, capital attempts a number of things that, each in their own way, fuel arguments that make labour time appear as irrelevant as the measure of capital's development. Looked at more carefully, however, each can be seen in a somewhat different light. To begin with, capital tries as much as possible to externalise its labour costs: to take a banal example (although not so banal if you are a former bank employee), by encouraging online and teller machine banking and discouraging over-the-counter customer service. As for our own work regimes, many of us find ourselves bringing more and more work home (or on the train, or in the car). More and more of us also seem to be on stand-by, accessible through the net or by phone. Added together, such strategies (which, to add to the messiness of it all, may well intersect with our own individual aspirations for greater flexibility) go a long way to help explain that blurring of the line between the 'work' and 'non work' components of our day that Negri decries. On the other hand, they also cast that boundary in light other than that of the collapse of labour time as the measure of value, one in which – precisely because the quantity of labour time is crucial to capital's existence – as much labour as possible comes to be performed in its unpaid form.

Secondly, in seeking to decrease labour costs within individual organisations, capital also reshapes the process through which profits are distributed on a sectoral and global scale. In a number of essays over the past 15 years, George Caffentzis has outlined the idea, first elaborated at some length in the third volume of Marx's *Capital*, that average rates of profit suck surplus value from labour-intensive sectors towards those with much greater investment in fixed capital:

> In order for there to be an average rate of profit throughout the capitalist system, branches of industry that employ very little labour but a lot of machinery must be able to have the right to call on the pool of value that

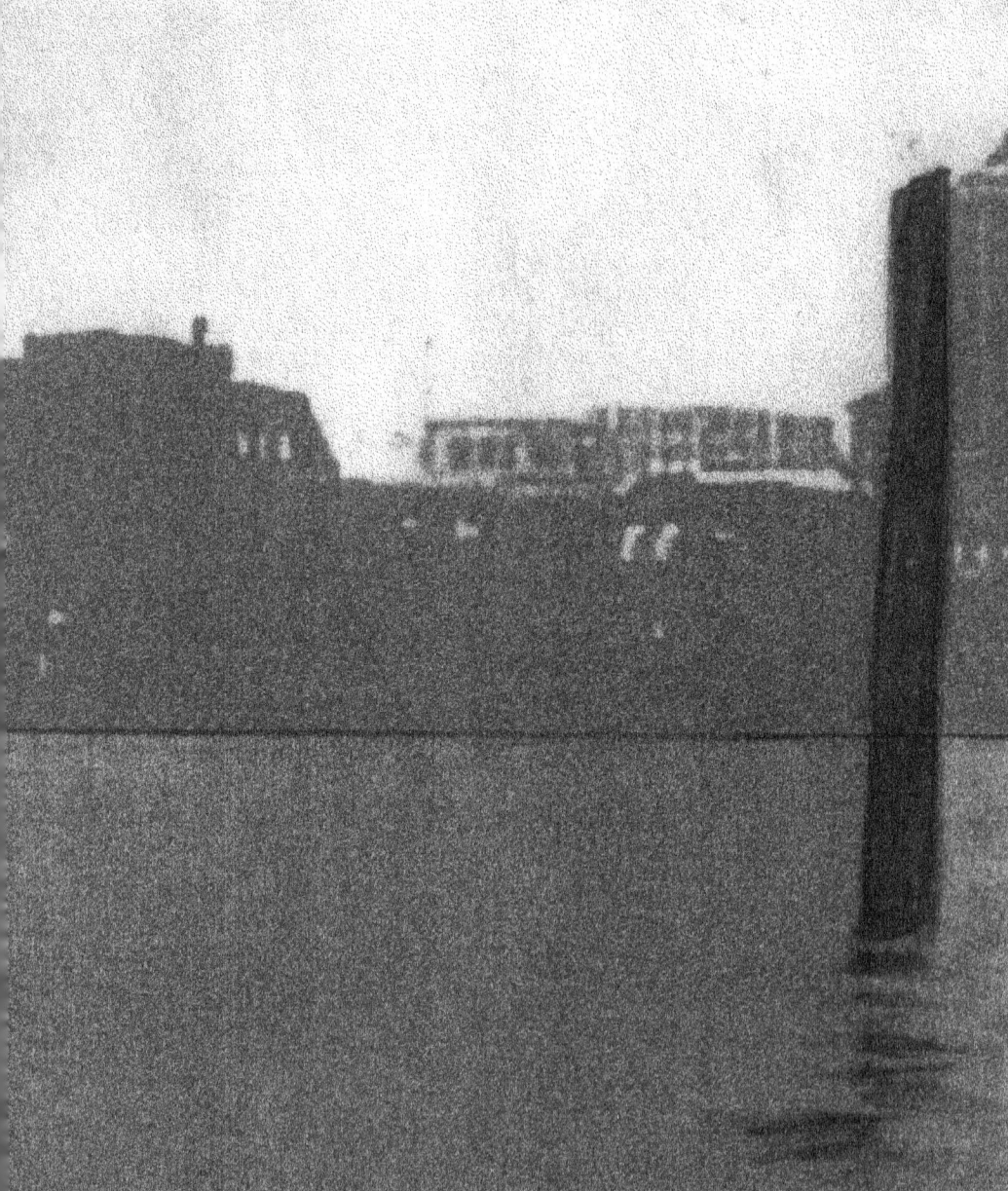

PIRATE WOMEN ON MOTORBOAT
'RIDDING THEMSELVES OF GOV. PAPERS'

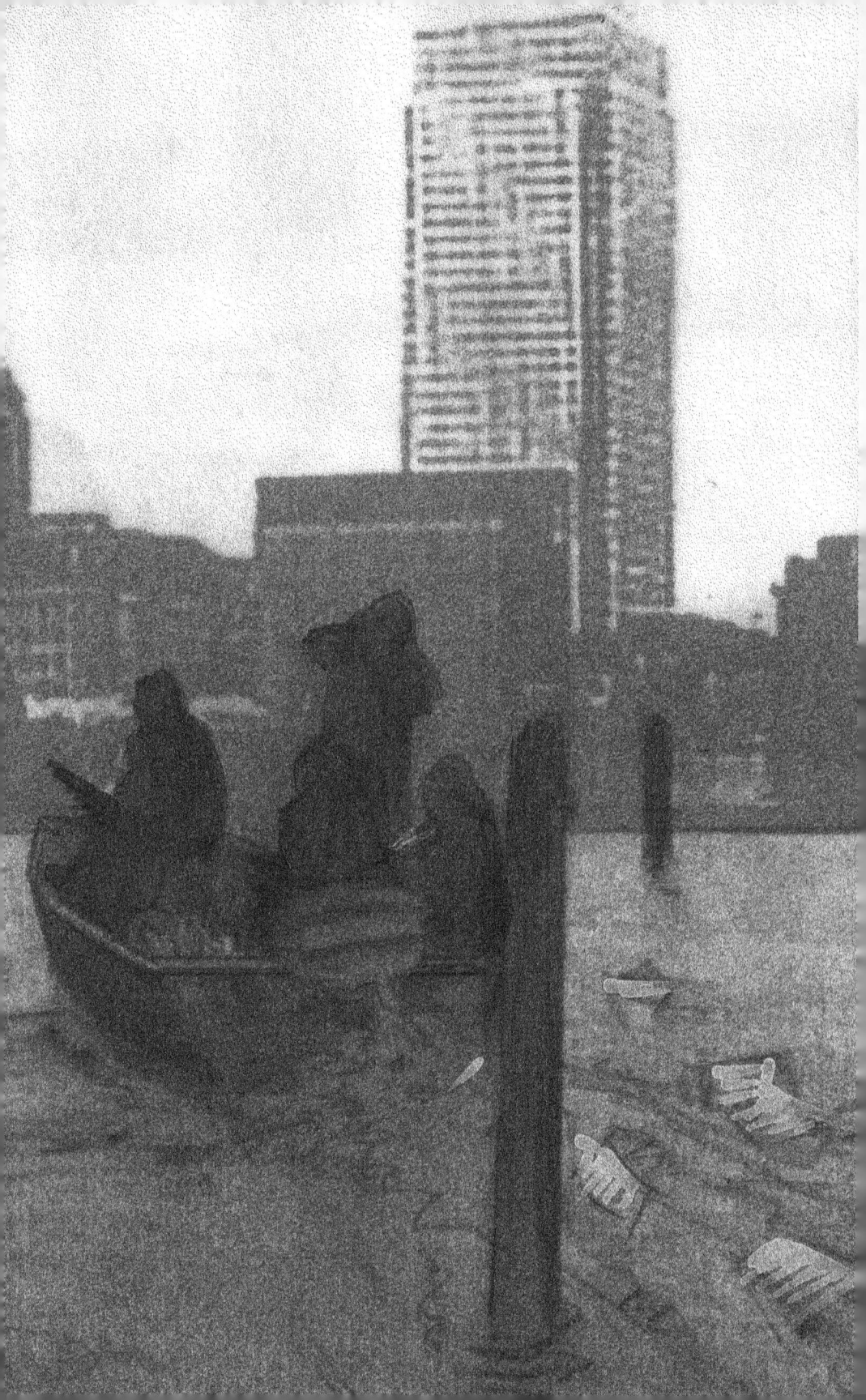

high-labour, low-tech branches create. If there were no such branches or no such right, then the average rate of profit would be so low in the high-tech, low-labour industries that all investment would stop and the system would terminate. Consequently, 'new enclosures' in the countryside must accompany the rise of 'automatic processes' in industry, the computer requires the sweat shop, and the cyborg's existence is premised on the slave.**24**

In this instance, if there *appears* to be no immediate correlation between the value of an individual commodity and the profit that it returns in the market, the answer may well be that there is none: the puzzle can only be solved by examining the sector as a whole, in a sweep that reaches far beyond the horizons of immaterial labour. Here too, it's a matter of which parameters we choose to frame our enquiry.

Thirdly, and following on from above, the division of labour in many organisations, industries and firms has reached the point where it is difficult – and probably pointless – to determine the contribution of an individual employee to the mass of commodities that they help to produce.**25** Again, this can foster the sense that the labour time involved in producing such commodities (whether tangible or not) is irrelevant to the value they contain. Marx, for his part, argued that the central question in making sense of all this was one of perspective:

> If we consider the aggregate *worker*, i.e. if we take all the members comprising the workshop together, then we see that their *combined activity* results materially in an *aggregate* product which is at the same time *a quantity of goods*. And here it is quite immaterial whether the job of a particular worker, who is merely a limb of this aggregate worker, is at a greater or smaller distance from the actual manual labour.**26**

In this regard, Ursula Huws' critique of notions of 'the weightless economy' deserves careful attention. Like Doug Henwood in his fierce deconstruction of the 'new economy',**27** Huws draws our attention back not only to the massive infrastructure that underpins 'the knowledge economy', but also to 'the fact that real people with real bodies have contributed real time to the development of these "weightless" commodities.'**28** As for determining the contribution of human labour within the production of immaterial products, Huws argues, that while this might 'be difficult to model, that 'does not render the task impossible'. Or, in David Harvie's words, 'every day the personifications of capital – whether private or state – make judgements regarding value and its measure' in their efforts 'to reinforc[e] the connection between value and work'; He adds:

the cyborg's existence is premised on the slave

Hardt and Negri may believe in the 'impossibility of power's calculating and ordering production at a global level', but 'power' hasn't stopped trying and the 'impossibility' of its project derives directly from our own struggles against the reduction of life to measure.**29**

OTHER LEADS?

Not long ago, Dr Woo pointed me to a presentation by Brian Holmes entitled 'Continental Drift Or, The Other Side of Neoliberal Globalisation'.**30** In large part, his talk is a reflection upon the arguments in Hardt and Negri's *Empire*, taking advantage of the hindsight provided by five years of events since the book's publication. For Holmes, many of the arguments advanced in *Empire* were important for challenging commonplace assumptions about how to make sense of the 'big picture' of global power relations, forcing a reconsideration of terms such as globalisation and imperialism. But if the book helped in clearing away certain misconceptions, it has not been nearly so successful in supplanting them with more adequate ways of seeing.

'Continental Drift' addresses a host of issues, but Holmes makes three points which have great relevance for our current discussion. First, a privileged focus upon 'immaterial labour' is increasingly unsatisfactory for efforts to understand what is happening within contemporary class composition. Second, global events since the publication of *Empire* cast doubt upon the usefulness of seeing capital's domination as a smooth space that lacks centre(s). And third, more attention has to be paid to the reasons why the world of finance has become such a crucial aspect of capital's rule in our time. Regarding the first point, Holmes offers some similar criticisms to those made by Dyer-Witheford. If the concept of immaterial labour is important for analysing certain kinds of work 'in the so-called tertiary or service sectors of the developed economies', talk of its hegemony can obscure not only 'the global division of labour' and thus 'the precise conditions under which people work and reproduce themselves', but also how 'they conceive their subordination and their possible agency, or their desires for change.' As for the second point, Holmes argues that global capitalism is better understood through the analysis of 'regional blocs' such as the European Union or the increasing engagement between China, Japan, and Southeast Asia. Finally, he believes that a far better understanding is needed of the role of money – and of finance above all – in capital's efforts to maintain its control at both the international and individual level (on this score, see also Loren Goldner's writings on fictitious capital).**31**

The richest explorations of regional blocs that I have encountered are those developed by 'world systems' analysts such as Immanuel Wallerstein, Giovanni Arrighi and Beverly Silver. Interestingly enough, their efforts to explain the emergence of a new cycle of global accumulation with its epicentre in Asia is intimately bound up with their attempt to understand why the expansion of money as capital has come so

'capitalism seeks to involve even the worker's personality within the production of value'

much to the fore over the past thirty years or so. For them, the predominance of financial expansion is symptomatic of a necessary phase in the cycle of accumulation when, as doubts mount concerning the profitability to be found within production, industries are relocated, unemployed capital and labour pile up, and 'a sharp acceleration of economic polarisation [occurs] both globally and within states'.**32** In recent times, Arrighi (who also penned one of the more considered reviews of *Empire*) has devoted much of his efforts to understanding the waning fortunes of the US state and capital within this process,**33** while Silver has concentrated upon the prospects facing contemporary labour in an age of capital flight.**34** The work of these authors (much of which is on the net) is well worth a look: in part for the challenges they offer to a number of radical orthodoxies, but also for the depth of analysis that they bring to their account of the conflicts between and within the forces of labour and capital today.

There is still a great deal to unravel in the issues touched upon here. All the same, there are some useful leads as to where to go next. For example, the current centrality of money as capital, with all the peculiarities that it entails, may offer another reason why it might *appear* that socially necessary labour time no longer has any bearing upon capital's existence as value in search of greater value. Speculative ventures – of which the past decade has been rife – seem to make money out of thin air. But in actuality, they do nothing to increase the total pool of value generated by capital. At best, they redistribute what already exists. More uncertainly, they seek to sidestep the sphere of production and instead make money 'from betting on the future exploitation of labour'.**35** In the meantime, debt continues to balloon, from the micro scale of individual and family credit cards, to the macro level of public sector budgets and current account deficits. Whatever the ingenious ways through which the burden of such debt is redistributed, the terms of the wager cannot be forestalled forever. When it is finally called in, things will become very interesting indeed. If nothing else, we may then find out at last whether, as Madonna sang:

> The boy with the cold hard cash
> Is always Mister Right, 'cause we are
> Living in a material world. ⤴

FOOTNOTES

1 Thanks to Hobo for telling me this story. Thanks too to Angela Mitropoulos and Nate Holdren for their helpful suggestions with this piece. All mistakes my own, etc.

2 For the best introduction to postworkerism see the Generation Online website http://www.generation-online.org

3 Negri, A. (1994) 'Oltre la legge di valore', *DeriveApprodi* 5-6, Winter

4 Lazzarato, M. (1996) 'Immaterial Labour', in P. Virno & M. Hardt (eds.) *Radical Thought in Italy: A Potential Politics*. Minneapolis: University of Minnesota Press, p.133

5 Ibid, p.137

6 Ibid, p.136

7 Hardt, M. & Negri, A. (2000) Empire. Cambridge: Harvard University Press, p.30

8 Ibid, p.292

9 Ibid, p.290

10 Henwood, D. (2003) After the New Economy. New York: New Press, pp.184-5

11 Dyer-Witheford, N. (2005) 'Cyber-Negri: General Intellect and Immaterial Labour', in Murphy, T. & Mustapha, A. (eds.) *Resistance in Practice: The Philosophy of Antonio Negri*. London: Pluto Press, pp.151-55

12 Hardt & Negri (2000), op. cit., p294

13 Huws, U. (2003) *The Making of a Cybertariat*. New York: Monthly Review Press, p.138

14 Hardt, M. & Negri, A. (2004) *Multitude: War and Democracy in the Age of Empire*. New York: Penguin, p.109

15 Ibid, p.114

16 Ibid, p.115

17 Huws, op. cit, p.130

18 Bologna, S. (1992) 'Problematiche del lavoro autonomo in Italia (I)', *Altreragioni* 1, June, pp.20-1

19 Ibid, pp.22-4

20 Caffentzis, G. (2005) 'Immeasurable Value?: An Essay on Marx's Legacy', *The Commoner* 10, Spring/Summer

21 Marx, K. (1973) *Grundrisse*. Hardmondsworth: Penguin, p.705

22 Negri, (1994), op. cit., 28

23 Marx, op. cit., 706

24 Caffentzis, G. (1997) 'Why Machines Cannot Create Value or, Marx's Theory of Machines', in J. Davis, T. Hirschl & M. Stack (eds.) *Cutting Edge: Technology, Information, Capitalism and Social Revolution*. London: Verso

25 Harvie, D. (2005) 'All Labour is Productive and Unproductive', *The Commoner* 10, Spring/Summer

26 Marx, K. (1976) 'Results of the Immediate Process of Production', now in *Capital* Vol. I. Hardmondsworth: Penguin, quoted in H. Cleaver, H. Cleaver (2001) *Reading Capital Politically*. Second Edition. Antithesis

27 Henwood, op. cit.

28 Huws, op. cit., pp.142-3

29 Harvie, op. cit., pp.151-154

30 Holmes, B. (2005) 'Continental Drift Or, The Other Side of Neoliberal Globalization', http://info.interactivist.net/article.pl?sid=05/09/27/131214&mode=nocomment&tid=9

31 Goldner, L. (2005) 'China In the Contemporary World Dynamic of Accumulation and Class Struggle', http://home.earthlink.net/~lrgoldner/china.html, and L. Goldner (2005) 'Fictitious Capital and the Transition out of Capitalism', http://home.earthlink.net/%7Elrgoldner/program.html

32 Wallerstein, I. (2003) *The Decline of American Power*. New York: The New Press, p.275

33 Arrighi, G. (2005a) 'Hegemony Unravelling – 1', *New Left Review* 32, March-April, and, Arrighi, G. (2005b) 'Hegemony Unravelling – 2', *New Left Review* 33, May-June

34 Silver, B. (2002) *Forces of Labour*. Cambridge: Cambridge University Press

35 Bonefeld, W. & Holloway, J. (1995) 'Conclusion: Money and Class Struggle', in Bonefeld, W. & Holloway, J. (eds.) *Global Capital, National State, and the Politics of Money*. New York: St. Martin's Press, pp.213-4

Steve Wright <pmargin@optusnet.com.au> works at Monash University and is the author of *Storming Heaven: Class Composition and Struggle in Italian Autonomist Marxism*, London: Pluto Press

FREEDOM'S STANDARD ADVANCED?

CREATIVE COMMONS AND THE FREE SOFTWARE MOVEMENT

Just how many licences do we need to preserve freedom? Benjamin Mako Hill uses his experience in the development of Free Software to address the weakness of Creative Commons licenses

Creative Commons (CC) advocates such as Lawrence Lessig have become fixtures on panels discussing Free Libre and Open Source Software (FLOSS). Frequently they are seen as representatives of the growing movement to translate the principles of free software to the world beyond code. Creative Commons advocates, directors, and supporters increasingly describe the project as an attempt to apply the principles of free software, appropriately adapted, to less technical forms of creative expression like music, writing, and the visual arts.

Comparisons between CC and free software are hardly coincidental. The CC website proudly describes the inspiration for the project as, in part, 'the Free Software Foundation's GNU General Public License (GNU GPL).' Many of the minds behind CC (Lawrence Lessig, James Boyle, and others) made important contributions to legal and philosophical discussions of the free software movement before starting CC.

However, while the GNU GPL is FLOSS's most famous legal artifact, free software existed as a concept, as a movement, as code, and as licences before the GPL. As the GPL is revised and replaced, free software remains unchanged.[1] There are many free software licences and most look little like the GPL.

Free software's fundamental document is Richard Stallman's Free Software Definitions (FSD).[2] At its core, the FSD lists four freedoms:

The freedom to run the program, for any purpose;
The freedom to study how the program works, and adapt it to your needs;
The freedom to redistribute copies so you can help your neighbour;
The freedom to improve the program, and release your improvements to the public, so that the whole community benefits.

When a piece of software's licence provides these freedoms, the software is considered free software. When a piece of software's licence does not, it is not free. A requirement for attribution does not violate the four freedoms; hence, a licence requiring attribution can be free. A non-commercial use clause restricts the first freedom; as a result, licences barring commercial use are considered non-free, for better or for worse. After these fundamental freedoms are satisfied, FLOSS is licence agnostic.

Free software advocates have been able to use the free software definition as the rallying point for a powerful social movement. Free software, like the concept of freedom in any freedom movement, is something that one can demand, something that one can protest for, and something that one can work toward. Working toward these goals, freeand open source software movements have created the GNU/Linux operating system and billions of lines of freely available computer code.

For the CC founders and many of CC's advocates, FLOSS's success is a source of inspiration. However, despite CC's stated desire to learn from and build upon the example of the free software movement, CC sets no defined limits and promises no freedoms, no rights, and no fixed qualities. Free software's success is built upon an ethical position. CC sets no such standard.

At the core of most CC licences are a hodge-podge of pick-and-choose (and often incompatible) features that can include prohibitions on commercial use, the requirement to release and redistribute derivative works freely, the requirement to retain attribution, and a blanket ban on derivative versions altogether. The only quality common to all of these licences was that verbatim copies would always be distributable non-commercially. In other words, while works under CC licences may be licenced under any number of terms, all works allowed the non-commercial copying of unmodified versions without permission.

A new licence, the CC 'Sampling licence' or 'Recombo' licence – created in association with the band Negativland and the Brazilian music legend (and Minister of Culture) Gilberto Gil – prohibits even verbatim distribution while allowing for commercial and non-commercial sampling. Another new licence allows for a broad range of freedoms – but only for those living in the developing world.

It is important to note that every CC licence is aimed at a particular problem and

Creative Commons licences are designed to give artists choice. This is not freedom in the sense that the term is used in Free Software

addresses a particular need. A blanket restriction on commercial use and derivative works opens the door to many of the most widespread models for financial sustainability in the art and culture industries today. The risks of lawsuits over sampling and the onerous process of requesting permission has a real silencing effect that the Recombo licence is intended to address. The Developing Nations licence addresses a real global imbalance in the way international IP is structured. Each new licence exists for a good reason. But this is not the model that has made free software successful.

Creative Commons licences are designed to give artists choice. Lessig personally describes how Creative Commons, 'gives creators the freedom to choose how their works are used.' This is not freedom in the sense that the term is used in free software.

Until relatively recently, CC stood, and could act as a nexus, for a social movement focused on the requirement for verbatim non-commercial use of artistic works. A low bar in the minds of some, especially in comparison to free software, but a de facto bar nonetheless. The new Recombo and Developing Nations licences remove even that. While free software has succeeded by building a social movement for the idea of freedom, CC refuses to set any such limit.

Instead, CC's inability to represent even a minimal attachment to any defined spirit of sharing is apparent each time someone approaches the CC board with a real problem and an

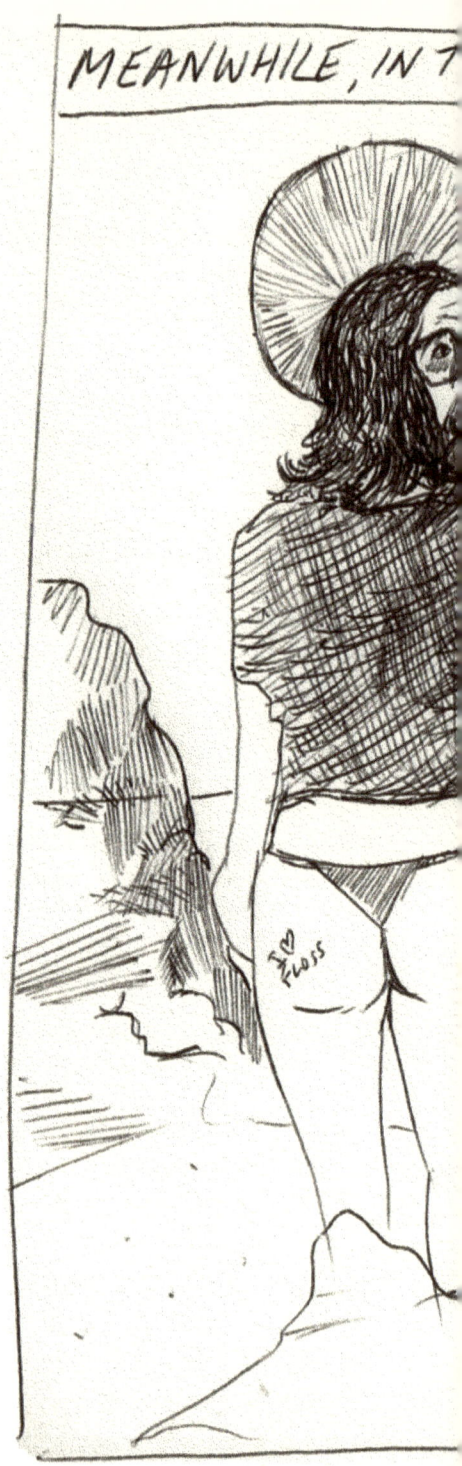

MEANWHILE, IN T

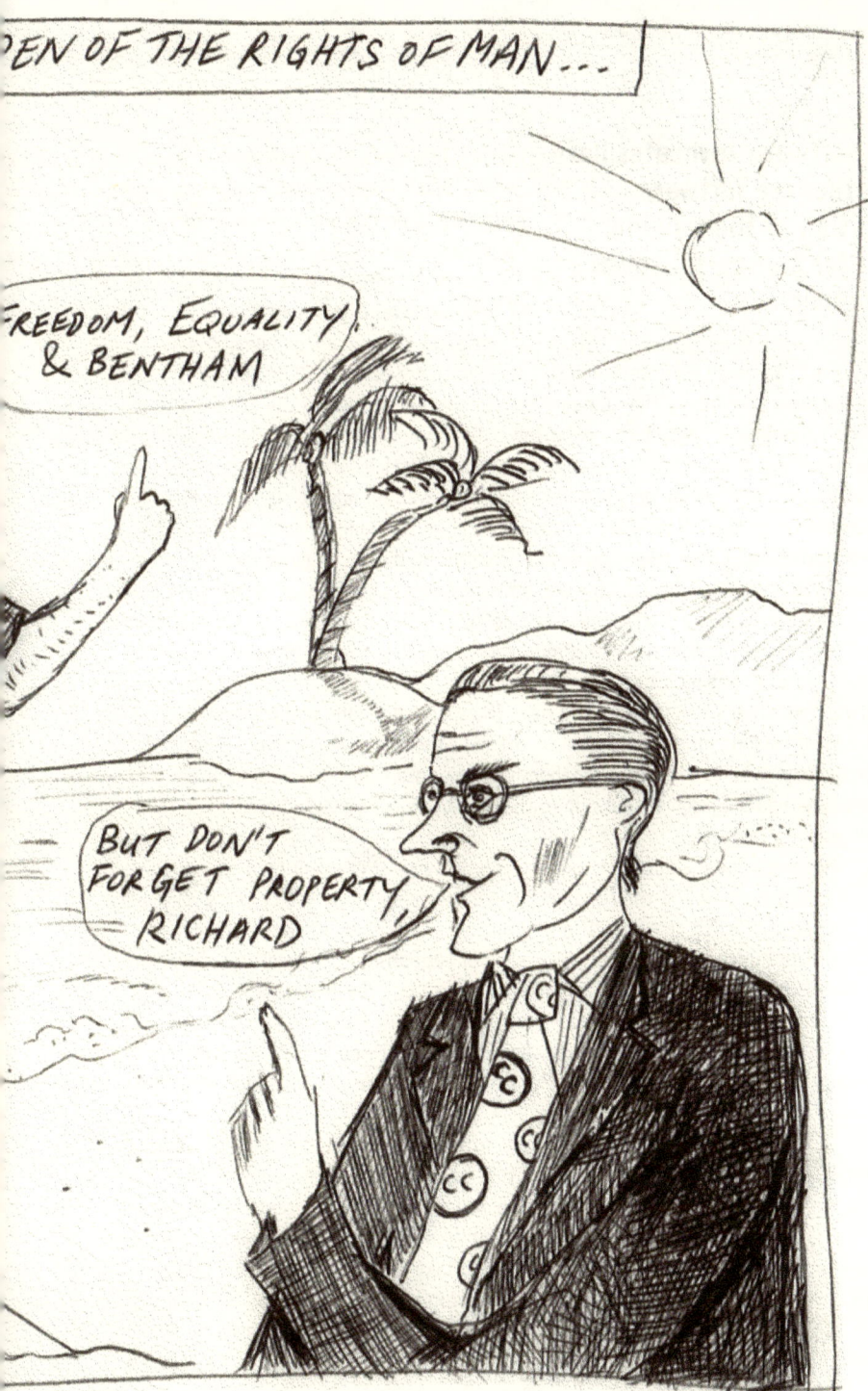

Image ▷ Benedict Seymour

Free software advocates have used the free software definition as the rallying point for a powerful social movement

interest in distributing their work under a licence that is more restrictive than the most restrictive CC licence but also less restrictive than the status quo.

Had CC followed a model similar to that of free software, they would have drawn a line in the sand. 'This is a Commons film. That film is not.' It would have sent a clear message that making a CC document is more difficult than convincing the CC board to add another licence to the CC website. By drawing this line, CC would be taking the risk that not as many individuals would be able or willing to use CC licences and that some injustices and imbalances might not be addressed by their project. Non-participation, even en masse, was a risk Richard Stallman was willing to take in the pursuit of more freedom for software. Ultimately, users of the GNU/Linux operating system created by the social movement he initiated have his stubbornness to thank for the consistent level of software freedom they enjoy.

To be sure, many programmers and software companies are uncomfortable with the freedoms required by the FSD. Programmers are welcome to release applications under a licence that prohibits terrorists, fascists, or pacifists from using their software but their software won't be free. There are very good and thoughtfully considered reasons for each freedom in the FSD; there may also be very good and thoughtfully considered reasons for choosing not to use them. free software draws a line and leaves the final judgment calls up to the developers applying the licences and the users using the software.

Not every programmer has to write free software. Not every programmer does. But if coders want to call their project 'free software' or 'open source,' they must pass the bar set in the FSD and OSD. If a programmer wants their software included in Debian, listed in the free software Directory, or supported by SourceForge, free software's core freedoms must exist for their users. As a result, few coders write 'almost free' software today while, proportionately, many more did two decades ago. With Creative Commons there is no bar and no essential freedom. As a social movement, CC has failed to take positions and set goals in the ways that made free software successful.

By no means is CC a bad thing – this article is distributed under a CC licence. Every CC licence clearly describes a right that cannot be taken for granted in contemporary copyright. With licences that declare an author's intentions, the need for lawyers and permission-asking is significantly minimized. CC licences are easy to understand and easy to apply. But by failing to take any firm ethical position and draw any line in the sand, CC is a missed opportunity.

Because CC has the support of influential intellectuals, and commands high profile institutional support, the creators of CC have had an opportunity to define a movement for the production of content in what they think is a better, more 'free', more 'open', or more 'common' manner. They have not done so.

When asked at the World Summit on the Information Society about non-commercial use clauses, Lessig said that he thought they were overused and frequently a bad idea. For whatever reasons, three-quarters of CC-licenced works prohibit commercial use.**3** Lessig provided licences and he hoped most creators' conservatism and fears would not get the better of them. Apparently, they did; artistic works under these licences are less accessible to a large number of creators.

Perhaps a literary or musical work can be free and open and restrict commercial use. Perhaps it can't. Inspired by the freeand open source software movement, one of the finest collections of legal and philosophical minds critical of contemporary intellectual property policy had the opportunity, foresight, and institutional and grassroots support to weigh in on a set of important issues – on either side. They did not. To this day, no widely discussed – much less widely accepted – definition of free, open, or common content exists.

This article is not an attempt to criticise the presence of non-commercial use clauses, or any of the other clauses, in Creative Commons' licences. Instead it is a criticism of the fact that there are no defined criteria by which any clauses can be categorically blocked. It is a criticism of the fact that there is no base level of freedom that every Creative Commons licence must provide. Creative Commons' website reads:

> Too often the debate over creative control tends to the extremes. At one pole is a vision of total control – a world in which every last use of a work is regulated and in which 'all rights reserved' (and then some) is the norm. At the other end is a vision of anarchy – a world in which creators enjoy a wide range of freedom but are left vulnerable to exploitation. Balance, compromise, and moderation – once the driving forces of a copyright system that valued innovation and protection equally – have become endangered species.

CC's goal of escaping a world of 'all rights reserved' is laudable, but they fail to describe what it will be replaced by except to say it will be better. While something slightly better is surely desirable, it might also be too little. Balance, compromise and moderation are certainly admirable and worthwhile goals; but undefined, unlimited, and unchecked, conservatism risks reducing CC's concept of balance toward little more than 'slightly better than the status quo.'

CC sets no defined limits and promises no freedoms, no rights, and no fixed qualities

While CC's licences are novel and effective tools, CC's 'freedom of choice' is hardly new; it forms the foundation upon

By failing to take any firm ethical position, CC is a missed opportunity

which copyright and all copyright licensing schemes work. It bears little resemblance, in scope, extent, or philosophical basis, to the Freedoms at the core of the free software movement. Lessig's cries for 'free culture' are not accompanied by a description of what freedoms – of use, of distribution, or of modification – free culture will provide.

CC has replaced what could have been a call for a world where essential rights are unreservable with the relatively hollow call for 'some rights reserved.' If the free software example is representative of how things might have been, the total amount of freedom the consumers of creative works enjoy in the future may be the price paid for CC's popularity.

It is not too late to discuss which rights should be unreservable in an era of free information. In fact, the rumblings of a movement to do just this have begun. Richard Stallman and others have withdrawn their support of Creative Commons and have expressed interest in supporting a 'free culture' movement with defined goals. Of course, the definition of freedom remains a slippery and controversial subject. Some, like Stallman, favour a model that treats functional works as distinct from artistic or political pieces. Others have argued persuasively against the division of commercial and non-commercial works from both principled and pragmatic positions. Consensus is hardly forthcoming.

But free software was hardly built two decades ago through consensus in the software development community. The success of the free software model was built through the hard work of Stallman and the GNU project, and the free and open source software communities. The movements' widespread popularity has been cemented through the benefits; pragmatic and principled, that only became evident with time. Whether in unison or cooperating in separate groups, it is time for those those of us that feel strongly about freedom to discuss, decide, and move forward with our own free information movement built upon a standard of freedom. When we have defined free information in terms of essential freedoms, a subset of Creative Commons works and a subset of Creative Commons licenses will provide tools and texts through which a social movement can be built. ⌐

FOOTNOTES

1 The current version of the GPL is the second version. A third version is currently being worked on by the Free Software Foundation

2 The Open Source Definition (OSD) was a verbatim copy of the Debian Free Software Guidelines (DFSG) that has diverged slightly over time – a checklist of qualities useful in determining compliance to the letter and spirit of the FSD. When the FSD is mentioned in this piece, it in almost all cases be substituted for either the OSD or the DFSG

3 Raw statistics of web links to the different licences are as good an indicator as we have of the licences' popularity. They are available at http://lists.ibiblio.org/pipermail/cc-fr/2005-February/000295.htm and elsewhere

Benjamin Mako Hill <mako@atdot.cc> is a technology and intellectual property researcher, activist, and consultant. He is currently working as a graduate researcher at the MIT Media Laboratory in the Electronic Publishing Group

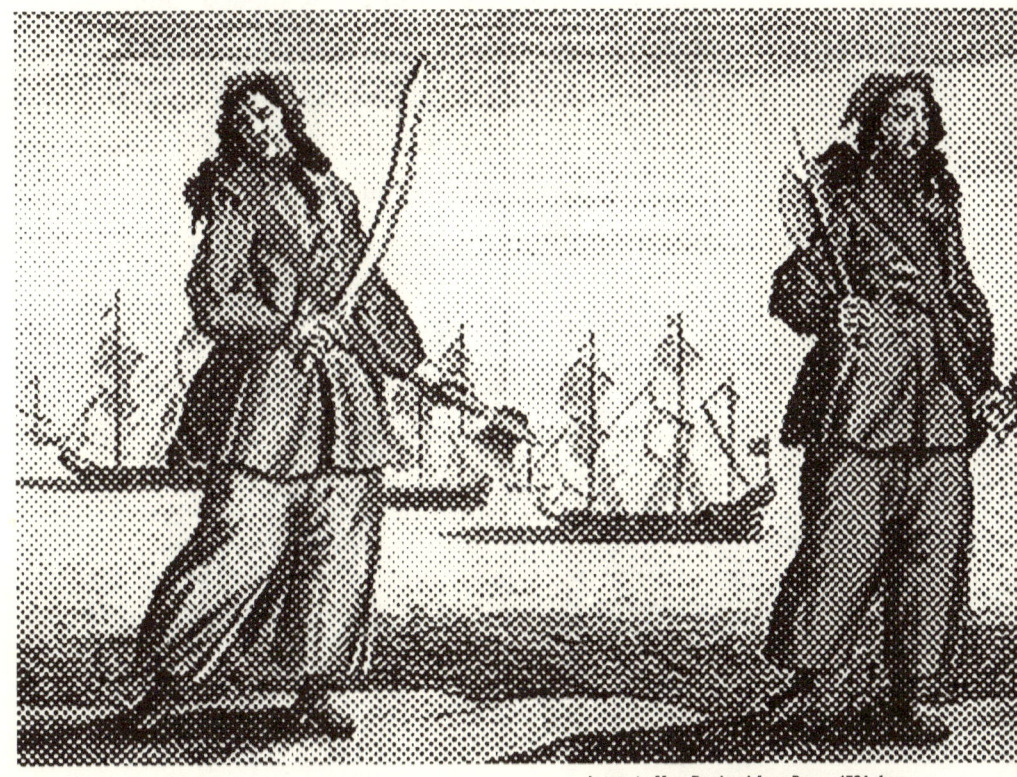

Image >‑ Mary Reed and Anne Bonny, 1724, from
A General History, by Captain Johnson

CHANGE OF THE CENTURY: FREE SOFTWARE AND THE POSITIVE POSSIBILITY

The much touted 'freedoms' of FLOSS are coming under increasing scrutiny as they are applied to contexts beyond their original formation. Is 'freedom as in speech' enough or are there other freedoms upon which the construction of the commons depends? Martin Hardie has worked extensively on an archeology of how the GNU/Linux operating system was developed, exposing the myths that are at its foundation. Here, he asks how the licensing of FLOSS operates within the constitution of Empire and locates in the new forms of 'producing in common' the means to reverse the proliferation of alternative law and instead affirm a true alternative to law

The key to the coming community is a positive possibility for a means against the destruction which the society of the spectacle wreaks on the common. The spectacle, the form that capital takes in today's globalised world, is the 'extreme form of the expropriation of the common' where 'our own linguistic nature comes back to us inverted'. It is on this terrain that we also find 'a positive possibility that can be used against it'.**1** In pursuing an archaeology of the Linux computer operating system and Free/Libre and Open Source Software (FLOSS), this positive possibility embodies in many ways my quarry.**2**

Despite its rhetoric of freedom, FLOSS does not directly address how it is captured within capital. What implications this has, and how, despite this, it may offer some possibility of life beyond the spectacle is absent from any debate. FLOSS sits comfortably within the Chestnut Cafe of *Nineteen Eighty Four* – a space where free spirits gathered for human contact and a sense of community allowing the possibility of open expression within the strictures of Orwell's repressive state.**3** The logic of FLOSS seems only to promise a new space for entrepreneurial freedom where we are never exploited or subject to others' command. The sole focus upon 'copyright freedom' sweeps away consideration of the processes of valorisation active within the global factory without walls.**4** It denies the necessary productive force that FLOSS provides for new forms of capital. In this Chestnut Cafe we are never subject to the machine of capital, we are machines of capital. The archetype of the Yankee inventor is teleported from its 19th century home through time into cyberspace. Free of the chains that bound us to the old system, we are now *vogelfrei* - free as the birds – to participate in the new global hi-tech economy.**5**

This lacuna in the logic of FLOSS brings up the difference between 'the common',**6** and 'the commons' of 'movements' such as the Creative Commons or FLOSS. The latter notion appears as a vast basin of things ready for consumption, facilitated by a commons constituted by law. The common takes on a somewhat different form. It does not concern individuals' ability to consume, but focuses upon relations, life and production in common. These two notions are as different as the village and the castle on the mountain of which Kafka wrote.**7**

FLOSS appears as a somewhat 'a-historical' form of freedom, in the sense that its logic locates its particular genealogy within a transcendental and ever present notion of foundational legal principle, rather than any material, historical or productive forces. Once read within a broader history of time machines – that is the quest for and development of both time coordination and time sharing, consolidated by the development of Unix – the freedom of FLOSS begins to appear in a different and more complex light than that promoted by its popular storytelling.

One noticeable theme in the history of time machines from the second half of the 19th century until today is how American notions of freedom, innovation and law feed into the global machine of sovereignty. Time coordination – the method of doing science that gave rise in part to the telecommunications infrastructure of modernity – appears as constitutive of a form of sovereignty and production that was confined within the bounds of the corporation and the nation state. Time sharing – the

'The common' does not concern individuals' ability to consume, but focuses upon relations, life and production in common

It is this telling of freedom and its deference to legal principle that seems to prevent us from encountering any positive possibility

method of interactive communal computing – points to an escape from these bounds. There appears an interface in this history where disciplines and practices of science, academia, law, military, sovereignty, governance, technology and mythology all become imbricated in each other. Here, power relations seem exposed, but at the same time they are hidden by law, popular stories and rhetoric. The task of excavating these relations is at once social, political, philosophical, technological, scientific and legal, therefore a biopolitical matter. This mixture appears as 'critical opalescence'– the point at which water and vapour no longer appear stable but flash back and forth between each other.**8** Critical opalescence is more than a mere metaphor. This is the consistent terrain on which we must seek to locate that elusive positive possibility: 'an ambiguous and uncertain zone', 'where law and fact seem to become undecidable.'**9**

THE LOGIC AND RHETORIC OF FREEDOM

Considering FLOSS within this zone, two primary conditions are exposed. On one hand, there are the technical conditions, the standards, that are necessary for the perpetuation of the particular technological, informational and communications infrastructure. On the other hand, these wires transmit a rhetoric and logic that purports to be counter cultural or a 'social movement', based upon the alternative use of legal principles. On investigation, this 'social movement' appears as broadly constructive of the imperial regime and its pursuance of the creation and sustenance of global market conditions.

The narrative of FLOSS and law extends particular American notions of innovation and Intellectual Property (IP) across the globe. This logic pilots the technological processes and their protrayal in popular storytelling, feeding back into the broader meaning of freedom in today's globalised world. It is this telling of freedom and its deference to legal principle that seems to prevent us from encountering any positive possibility.

Here law plays a unifying role. It presents a linear and unified story that masks over many of these signal flashes throughout the network. This approach reduces the contrast space of the enquiry by constraining both its presuppositions and the possible open alternatives. The discourse surrounding FLOSS is limited to only considering FLOSS as an alternative to forms of production bounded within the walls of the modern corporation and does not conceive of alternatives within the postmodern forms.**10** The detail of time sharing's history and critical opalescence defies both the linear approach and the sort of unification that the popular legal story portrays.

In the popular narrative, 'social movements' such as the Free Software Foundation (FSF), and its relations, the Creative Commons and the Electronic Frontier Foundation, act as 'patriots' and guardians of 'our' law and freedom.**11** This freedom is bound intimately with the logic of open democracy and with free and open markets. Witness pop professor and driving force behind the Creative Commons and Electronic Frontier 'movements', Lawrence Lessig, writing about his trip to the World Social Forum in Brazil in June 2005 under the banner of 'The People Own Ideas'.**12** Under the subheading 'Truly Free Market', Lessig gets to the core of this freedom: it is about technology, wealth, efficiency and growth. In rejuvenating a long standing U.S. Republican logic, this rhetoric seeks to justify the link between science and commercial prosperity, both national and global, by invoking a moral and political vision of freedom. In its shamelessly American vision: 'the kids at Porto Alegre' find their solace in a 'free culture'; an 'economy that governed creative industries for at least the first 186 years of the American republic.'**13**

The rhetoric of FLOSS proposes the technical device (the software) and the literary device (the licence) as machines of liberty and freedom. 'Free as in speech and not as in beer', locates FLOSS firmly within the tradition of U.S. constitutionalism. Lessig envisages the 'Future of Ideas' concerning 'our future' as a 'free society' in the age of the internet as a constitutional question – explicitly, then, as an American constitutional question determined by reference to the intent of 'our founders'.**14**

This spreading of American freedom is consistent with the imperial, supranational form of the global constitution, *Empire*, and its heritage in an American constitutional genealogy.**15** Consistent as well is the acknowledgment by the FSF of a licensing model that seeks to spread the application of U.S. Law globally in a liminal, or barely perceptible manner. I have recently sought to describe how the FSF's General Public License (GPL) takes on a form that is not law, but assumes the force of law within the state of exception.**16** The point here is that the FSF's perception of its legal model forms a part of the global encroachment of and by U.S. notions of freedom.

The GPL 'legal' model springs from the same constitutional heritage. The FSF does not recognise offshore or onshore legal environments, only a harmonised global copyright system that facilitates the distribution of its *'portfolio'* in the form of an internationalised GPL. This global licensing model seeks to evade the hard questions that arise in relation to the enforceability of the GPL under national legal principles through a combination of 'careful transactional planning', 'properly assembled code' and legal assignments of copyright from developers. Here a form of legal literature flashes U.S. legal principles through the wires

The Free Software Foundation's perception of its legal model forms a part of the global encroachment of and by U.S. notions of freedom

of the global ITC infrastructure which in turn become global principles apparently possessing the force of law. This liminal layer of *'code as law'***17** is not law as we knew it, but is something that has sprung up from the very depths of the system that is in construction. Licences, standards and stories comprise here a level of private ordering that hovers above formal law, but which is increasingly something that appears as having the force of law, and increasingly acts or is treated as if it actually was law. In the process these devices reconfigure our conception of law in line with the global machine.

LEGAL PRINCIPLE, PRACTICALITY AND THE EXCEPTION

The GPL does not assume the force of law because of some entrenched legality, or interpretation of legality in the way we conceive the rule of law in modernity. Neither does it gain its force because of some consistency with a particular tradition and interpretation of US copyright history. The GPL – the constitution of the Free Software community – remains valid at the threshold of the imperial constitution because it is consistent with the single logic of the global system. The point of validity or invalidity, or better still, the threshold point at which it assumes the force of law is marked by this functional fit. On the other hand, production in common, as distinct from the licence fetishism of the legally constituted commons of use and consumption of FLOSS, 'is anything but accountancy, compatibility and systematisation'.**18**

FSF legal counsel Eben Moglen, has commented upon what they envisage as the key to the GPL's success. He acknowledges that the lack of adversarial situations arising in respect of the GPL is in part because the large organisations which use the software are 'the major players building information technology systems' who 'understand the benefits from free software'. From this point of view the apparent force of law of the GPL receives its support not from legal principle or freedom, but from the very fact that major corporations involved in the ITC economy depend upon innovation and production occurring in a networked environment. Large corporations depend upon the existence of the factory without walls and the apparent force of law of the GPL is a result of its instrumentality in this environment.

Licences, standards and stories comprise here a level above formal law, but which appears to have the force of law, and increasingly acts or is treated as if it actually was law

The dependence of major corporations upon external innovation coincides with the embedding of FLOSS within environments of administration and governance. Moglen quite openly admits the desirability of embedding FLOSS within the global machine of administration as key to its long term success. ' ... Let me put it in the shortest possible way. Five years from now there's going to be not a government on earth that isn't using our stuff. There won't be a court system on earth that won't be using our stuff. Every judge will be aware of the fact that if the system breaks, his computer breaks. All I have to do is stand off until then.'

Being a part of the machine of governance, being embedded, and industry dependence, are the factors that shall ensure the GPL's 'success'. In embedding the licence and FLOSS these U.S. legal principles and notions of freedom are seeping through through the wires of the global ITC infrastructure. In turn they become global principles which appear to have the force of law. Embedding the technology and the legal literary device is the key to this force of law – as the system works, and becomes constructive of the global system, force of law self-executes.

The two strands of the FSF strategy, legal principle and corporate embedding should however still be considered within this genealogy of U.S. Constitutionalism. The 'freedom of the frontier' has been submitted to the constitution and has been organised around the 'kingdom of monetary circulation'. In this America, money has replaced the frontier and has re-organised power around financial capital.**19** Freedom of speech (and not as in beer) has become the breeding ground of the kingdom of money – the place where innovation takes place; rather than the threshold of the frontier. Freedom in this context is always capped by property and money. Here is the Hamiltonian concept of freedom in full view: property is essential to survival and the right to property is essential to autonomy.**20**

In the FSF's realist rational approach, legal principle takes a back seat, as does any notion of a new world which might have a social vision. With its realism, practicality, compatibility and systematisation, the GPL's functionality within the global system is central to its success: 'It is a very straight forward capitalist proposition and it is driven to success, not primarily by our cleverness or ingenuity, but by capitalism's need referred to in the original *Communist Manifesto*,to reinvent the mechanisms of its production all the time.'**21**

LOCATING POSSIBILITY

This bifurcated (schizo?) approach of the FSF reflects the imperial method of resorting to universal calls to justice whilst relying upon the state of exception as a tool of universal rule and command. The FSF genuflects to, and invokes the traditions of law and justice in a situation where the imperial machine prefers not to apply law. However at the foot of law's mountain, fact and law blur, and appear as simply life. This is the site of Galison's critical opalescence, of Agamben's state of exception'**22** it is the space where K stands below the Castle and prefers not to be entranced by the glitter of law above him.**23**

FLOSS finds itself within this space. However, rather than seeking any positive possibility within time sharing's method of production in common, it obscures these

The apparent force of the GPL receives its support not from legal principle or freedom, but from the fact that corporations involved in ITC depend upon networked innovation and production

processes by its deference to the maniacal glitter of law's promise. The focus on freedom in FLOSS does not concern, and even denies production and labour. It is this denial that blocks us from increasing our power in the face of the spectacle. Richard Stallman has recently written that the FSF is ' ... more concerned with the use of software than with its development for a specific practical reason: the use of software ... affects our freedom, whereas its development does not. Therefore, the details of the social system of use of software are directly important to us, in the way that the system of development isn't'.**24** This position is reflected by Lessig's view that 'how a resource is produced says nothing about how access to that resource is granted. Production is different from consumption'.**25**

This approach is directly at odds with the idea of the common, and of new forms of language and value produced within the circuits of immaterial labour. This factor, along with valorisation, opens up a reading of the genealogy of FLOSS as not one of a commons, but of privatisation. In the prehistory of FLOSS during the 1950's, AT&T and IBM relinquished the right to exclude in relation to their factories of patents and technical information. The knowledge of these quasi-public corporations was privatised in a micro-shift of antitrust settings. This shift coincided with a situation after the Second World War which required collaboration between corporations in order to construct a global ITC infrastructure. Thirty years on, when that infrastructure was well on its way to being up and running, it was not the corporation that relinquished the right to exclude, but the individual outside of the corporation. This relinquishing of a right to exclude or control the fruits of one's own labour, or the labour that produces in common with others, has been portrayed as freedom.

If legal practice and criticism is to go beyond its foundations and methods - beyond the confines of the State, and beyond reformism and alternative uses of law, it will need to find a 'new ontological setting of criticism'.**26** The GPL model is within the tradition of alternative uses of law and does not by itself point to any positive possibility, any new life beyond the shadow of law's mountain. In this regard Kirsty Best has noted that the FSF 'replicates elements of representative elitism and the leftists' metanarrative of utopia, discipline and planning', in its role as 'a form of avant-garde [leading] programmers and participants into the new utopia.'**27**

A 'new ontological setting of criticism' in this context entails a recognition of the state of exception as a flattened space that provides a basis for an alternative to law and not alternative law. It might be illuminated by the contrast between generality and repetition. In contradistinction to generality, repetition is the application of a particular idea or conduct to different circumstances – or better, a necessary and justified conduct only in relation to something irreplaceable. Generality exists 'as an empty form of difference, an invariable form of variation', which, as law, 'compels its subjects to illustrate it only at the cost of their own change.'**28** A new critical setting will have to reject the general, the rule to be applied to facts across the board, for the repetition of a means of acting, of a behaviour.**29**

One way of thinking about law as a means without ends,**30** might be by reference to equity's tradition.**31** Equity provides a fertile thinking ground for the organisation of FLOSS production.**32** As an exceptional power in itself, equity bears some of the traits of repetition. It is not about rules, but about an idea, a behaviour. It looks to substance, over form; it regards as done what ought to have been done. One who seeks equity must come with clean hands, they must have done equity themselves to be entitled to its relief.**33**

In the logic and rhetoric of FLOSS, the door to justice appears as an end, as a goal manifested by the referring back to legal principle, in a situation where although that principle no longer generally applies, it manages to maintain the fiction of law's transcendence. The door in this way holds out the promise that by genuflecting to law we will somehow manage to return to the glory days of its founders. But in fact, we can only pass through the door when it is is closed. That is when we recognise that the common – that which we produce in common – is a constitutive power, and not the commons of consumption constituted by a law or a deference to legal principle. It is when we no longer seek an end in the fatal attraction of transcendental law and the phantasmagoria of its rotten (although in so many other cases irresistible) promises that the door will remain closed. Only then may we be able to pass beyond it, to a life of means and ethics in the village below its decaying façade.

Thanks to Ornette Coleman for the title

FOOTNOTES

1 Giorgio Agamben, *The Coming Community*, Theory Out of Bounds Volume 1, University of Minnesota Press, 2001, p. 80

2 To come to grips with this quarry it is necessary to consider how what is produced in Common is subsequently valorised within the spectacle of daily life. There is no space here to examine how FLOSS is valorised but only to outline why organisations such as the FSF and CC ignore this aspect of production. In a work in progress I address these issues in the context of the development and dissemination of the Unix time sharing computer system. See: http://openflows.org/~auskadi/nix1.pdf

3 Kathy Bowrey, *Law and Internet Cultures*, Cambridge University Press, 2005, p. 81

4 Martin Hardie, *The Factory without Walls*, http://openflows.org/~auskadi/factorywoutwalls.pdf

5 Karl Marx, *Capital Volume One*, Part VIII Primitive Accumulation, p. 896. See also Michael Hardt and Antonio Negri, *Empire*, pp. 157-159, and Gilles Deleuze and Felix Guattari, *Anti-Oedipus*, p.225

6 Agamben's expression 'the common' bears considerable similarity to that which Hardt and Negri use concerning production 'in common' and rather than trying to split hairs between their approaches what interests me more is what their conceptions have share in contradistinction to the idea of 'the commons'

7 Franz Kafka, *The Castle*, in *The Complete Novels*, Vintage, 1999. This passage from Kafka is central to Giorgio Agamben's discussion of the relation of law to life in his recent book, *State of Exception*, Chicago University Press, 2005

8 Peter Galison, *Einstein's Clocks, Poincaré's Maps, Empires of Time*, Hodder and Stoughton, 2003, pp. 26 ff. Cited in Martin Hardie, 'Time Machines and the Constitution of the Globe' http://openflows.org/~auskadi/timemachines.pdf

9 Giorgio Agamben, *State of Exception*

10 Manuel Delanda, *Intensive Science and Virtual Philosophy*, Continuum, London, 2004, p 130

11 Free Software Foundation, http://www.fsf.org/. See also the free software definition: http://www.fsf.org/licensing/essays/free-sw.html, and philosophy: http://www.gnu.org/philosophy/philosophy.html. Creative Commons, http://creativecommons.org/. Note the page 'Founders Copyright': http://creativecommons.org/projects/founderscopyright/, 'The Framers of the U.S. Constitution understood that copyright was about balance — a trade-off between public and private gain, society-wide innovation and creative reward.' Electronic Frontier Foundation, http://www.eff.org/. Note the page 'Our Mission': http://www.eff.org/mission.php, 'If America's founding fathers had anticipated the digital frontier, there would be a clause in the Constitution protecting your rights online, as well. ... Instead, a modern group of freedom fighters was necessary to extend the original vision into the digital world. ... That's where the Electronic Frontier Foundation comes in. ... Just as patriots fought for liberty and freedom, we fight measures that threaten basic human rights. Only the dominion we defend is the vast wealth of digital information, innovation, and technology that resides online. ... '

12 Lawrence Lessig, 'The People Own Ideas!', TechnologyReview.com, http://www.technologyreview.com/articles/05/06/issue/feature_people.1.asp

13 Lawrence Lessig, 'The People Own Ideas!', http://www.technologyreview.com/articles/05/06/issue/feature_people.7.asp Regarding the liberation of the globe by American notions of freedom, see Lawrence Lessig's map of the spread of the Creative Commons, http://www.lessig.org/blog/archives/002952.shtml. 'As of Thursday, (June 8 2005)' he writes, 'the current spread of Creative Commons. The green are countries where the project has launched. The yellow are close. The red is yet to be liberated'

14 Lawrence Lessig, *The Future of Ideas*, Vintage, 2002; Martin Hardie, 'Foreigner in a Free Land?', *Sarai Reader* 4, Sarai, India, 2004, pp. 384-387 http://www.sarai.net/journal/04_pdf/51martin_hardie.pdf

15 Michael Hardt and Antonio Negri, *Empire*, pp.160 ff

16 'Liminal Law and the Exceptional Art of Linux Licensing', paper presented at the Critical Law Conference, Kent University, Canterbury, U.K., 2 September 2005

17 Editor's note: the GPL is made available in both human and machine readable form

18 Antonio Negri, 'Alma Venus: Love', in *Time for Revolution*, Continuum, 2003, p. 222

19 Martin Hardie, 'Foreigner in a Free Land?', pp. 384-387

20 Ibid. pp. 390-391

21 Eben Moglen interviewed by Kathy Bowrey available at: http://auskadi.civiblog.org/blog/archives/2005/6/25/972325.html

22 This is also Negri's Kairos – time as qualitative duration; it is also the site of the passage described by Deleuze 'a lived phenomenon, ... It is increase or decrease of my power, even infinitesimally.' Deleuze, Gilles. 'Lecture Transcripts on Spinoza's Concept of Affect', http://www.goldsmiths.ac.uk/csisp/PDF/deluze_spinoza_affect.pdf

23 Franz Kafka, *The Castle*

24 Richard M. Stallman, [Upd-discussion list] Paper: 'Digital property', Sabine Nuss, NY, NY, April 12-14, 2002, Sat, 06 Aug 2005, http://lists.essential.org/pipermail/upd-discuss/2005q3/001255.html

25 Lawrence Lessig, *The Future of Ideas* p. 13

26 Antonio Negri, 'Postmodern Global Governance and The Critical Legal Project', *Global Jurist Advances Volume* 1, Issue 3, 2001

27 Kirsty Best 'The Cultural Politics of the Open Software Movement and the Gift Economy' *International Journal of Cultural Studies*, Vol. 6, No. 4, (2003), pp.449-470

28 Gilles Deleuze, *Difference and Repetition*, Columbia University Press, 1995, pp 2-3

29 Repetition 'is by nature transgression and exception, always revealing a singularity opposed to particulars subsumed under laws, a universal opposed to the generalities which give rise to laws.' Gilles Deleuze, *Difference and Repetition*, p.5

30 In *Means without End*, Giorgio Agamben argues for a politics of pure means that is not altogether dissimilar to that projected by Walter Benjamin, 'politics is the sphere neither of an end in itself nor of means subordinated to an end;

rather, it is the sphere of a pure mediality without end intended as the field of human action and of human thought' Giorgio Agamben *Means without End: Notes on Politics* Translated by Vincenzo Binetti and Cesare Casarino, Minnesota, 2000

31 'A branch of law that developed alongside common law in order to remedy some of its defects in fairness and justice', *The Oxford English Dictionary*

32 Kathy Bowrey, *Law and Internet Cultures*, pp.95-97, and Martin Hardie, 'The Shape of Law to Come?' http://openflows.org/~auskadi/shapeoflaw.html

33 Martin Hardie, 'The Shape of Law to Come?'

Martin Hardie <martin.hardie@gmail.com> has managed bands, worked in Aboriginal Art centres, been a solicitor, a barrister, an advisor to various members of the former East Timorese resistance, and a university lecturer. He is currently researching a Doctor of Laws at the University of New South Wales, Sydney and spends his time between the Basque Country and Mozambique. His ambition is to become the archetype of life within communism; at the break of dawn a cyclist, during the day a cook, cyber-conspiracist and correspondent, in the afternoons a student and philosopher and, at nights, simply pleasant company. See his homepage at http://auskadi.tk/

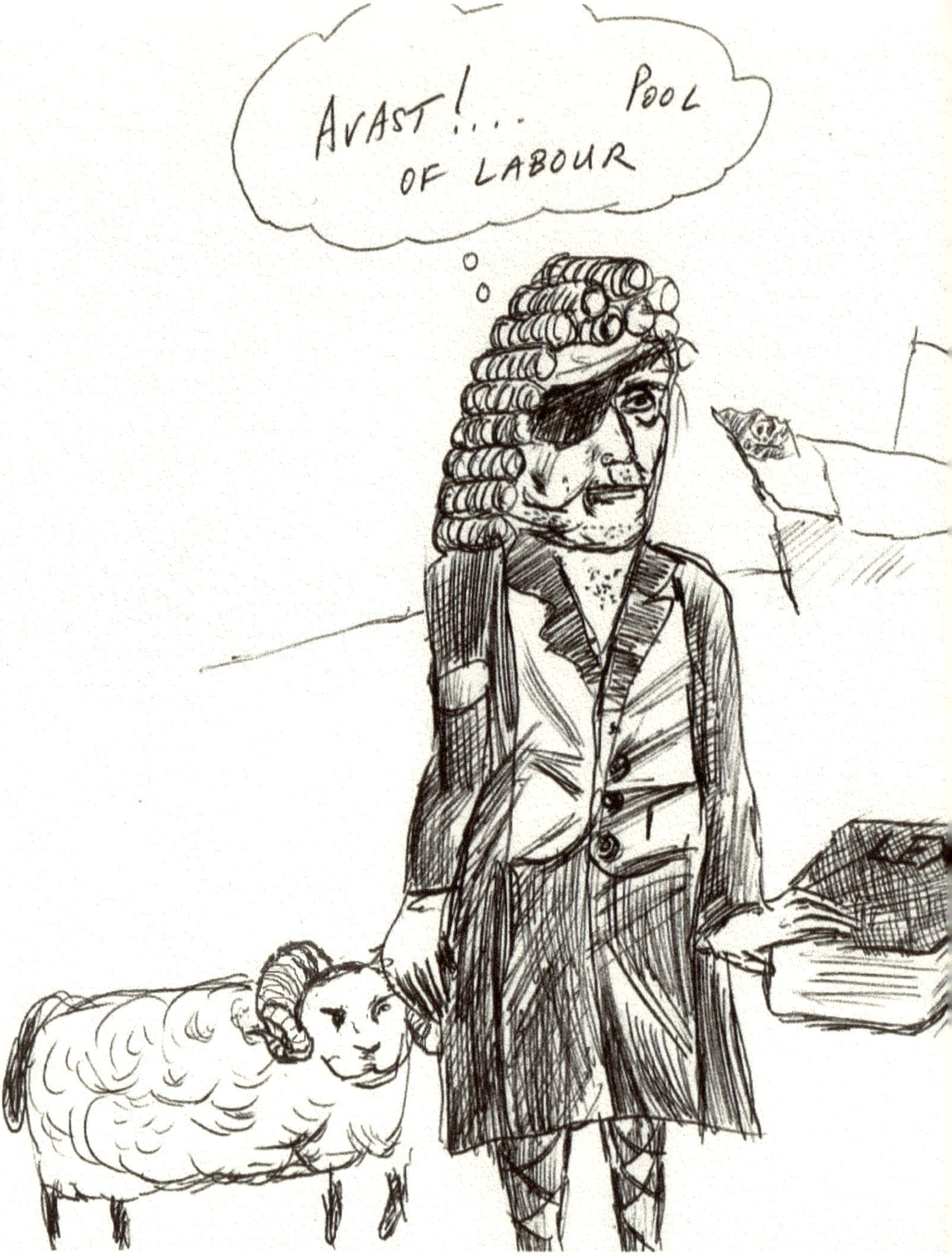
AVAST!... POOL OF LABOUR

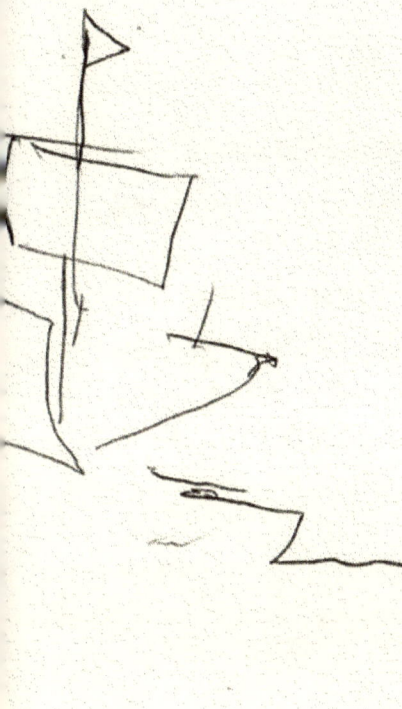

COPY THAT FLOPPY!

The Pirate Bay, a tracker website based in Sweden, has become the most popular BitTorrent site in the world and now receives more daily hits than CNN. The Pirat Byran (Pirate Association) is its sister organisation, and promotes information piracy and its culture through discussions, media advocacy and legal advice. *Mute* **talked to Palle Torsson of Pirat Byran about filesharing culture in Sweden and the 'grey commons'**

Mute: The Pirate Bay is one of the most popular BitTorrent trackers, could you tell us about how The Pirate Bay and Pirat Byran came about?

PT: Pirat Byran was born in 2003 from an integrated internet radio broadcast community and IRC channel populated by the Swedish hacker community and Demo scene. PB was initiated to support the free copying of culture and launched the BitTorrent tracker and website: The Pirate Bay. When TPB expanded to become the biggest BitTorrent tracker in the world it was natural for them to split up into two different entities. PB has evolved into a community and an information site in Swedish with news, forums, articles, resources and a shop and has to date over 50,000 members. PB organises events, appears in debates, writes and answers questions about IP and filesharing. TPB had recently gone through a major internationalisation and can now be browsed in many languages, from Mandarin to Icelandic.

A big crowd came, something like 800 people, with banners like: 'No Software Patents', 'Sharing is caring' and 'All Your Base [Stations] Belong to Us'

Mute: I read some time ago a report on Interactivist http://linkme2.net/5o about filesharing protests in Sweden. I understand you spoke at the demo?

PT: Yes, but the speech I made took most of my energy. It was the second year when internet lovers, filesharers and pirates gathered in Stockholm to express their fight for internet freedom. There was music and three speakers talking about the transgression of IP law and creativity. A hand to hand copyswap was extended to a coffin where you could place and share CDs. A big crowd of something like 800 people assembled with banners declaring things like: 'No Software Patents', 'Sharing is Caring' and 'All Your Base [Stations] Belong to Us.' This aggressively humorous attitude is something that characterises the movement in Sweden. One beautiful example is the letter written by TPB in response to legal threats and the request by big companies like Microsoft, DreamWorks and Warner Bros, to remove copyrighted material: http://thepiratebay.org/legal.php.

Last year the transgression of IP law spurred a copy riot in Sweden; people from right to left have woken up and spoken out on the subject. This escalated further when Sweden's anti-piracy lobby organisation, Antipiratbyran (APB), raided Swedish ISPs claming they hosted unlicensed material. The raid was conducted in an unlawful manner and it was discovered APB had paid an infiltrator for several months to upload copyright-protected material and place hardware at the ISP.

This spawned a public outcry and the lawyer and spokesperson for APB, Henrik Ponten, received hate-SMS, including death threats, from a lot of angry kids. The homepage of APB was hacked by a group that called themselves Angry Young Hackers and mails between people from APB were published showing that APB were also infiltrated. In response PB has pressed charges against APB for their different unlawful actions. And APB was told by Swedish authorities to withdraw the most aggressive of these threats to protect their own integrity.

The demonstration was mostly a great celebration with a lot of different people sharing and also making connections. The slogans at the demonstration were: 'Copy me – we will continue to copy everything', 'Don't touch our internet' and 'Welfare begins at 100 Mbit'. The counter-allegations against the anti-pirate organisation APB for the action and the raid at the Swedish ISP Bahnhof was ready at that time and was handed to the police.

Mute: As I understand it Sweden has yet to sign European agreements on copyright law. Does this make it a 'zone of exception' as far as the increasingly aggressive policing of IP is concerned?

PT: No, but for a long time it was legal to download for personal use. Now the EU [Copyright] Directive is implemented and in force in Sweden (as of 1 July), even

I always appropriate, borrow or steal others people's work to make something new. I live in, I distribute with, and take from the circulation of information

though there have not yet been any cases resulting from the new law. This 'zone of exception' comes rather from the fact that people accept and live with filesharing, the police don't have the will, priorities or resources to criminalise kids. TPB and PB is a concrete, factual and living example of this, among other things. This zone of exception is important and natural for this generation and is not something that will change any time soon.

Mute: What is the bigger picture behind these protests? Was this the first public act of disobedience in opposition to the new laws or are there events that have prefigured this one?

PT: PB has a broad political base, from high-tech autonomists to free libertarians. A group based in Malmo called The Street Action looks upon filesharing as digital class struggle and organises public copyswaps inside shopping malls in order to desecrate the commodity. And there are several other interesting projects based on disobedience in Sweden, of which my favourites are Planka.nu and Snatta.nu. Planka.nu is a site for free subway riding and runs a fund to which you can subscribe and get your money back in case you get caught and fined. Snatta.nu is a site for shoplifting culture.

Mute: You spoke of finding the 'power to strike again', at what forms of power are you directing these attacks and through what means?

PT: I always appropriate, borrow or steal others people's work to make something new. I live in, distribute, and take from the circulation of information. The configurations of the medial structures in which this information exists is the pipeline in which I work. The motivation for my work is to try to intervene in this structure and to create an alternative work space, basically to make my becoming a place were I am free to appropriate again.

There is an endless amount of targets to strike that oppose our way of living, but right now it feels important to build the alternative playground of sharing and gift culture. The confrontation comes naturally in the process of exploring these grounds. The primary means for this is collaboration and exchange of knowledge. I think hacking that involves hardware modification will become more important because the industry understands they have lost the information battle and are moving towards the protection of hardware. This means that it will be important to

It was discovered Sweden's anti-piracy lobby organisation had paid an infiltrator for several months to upload copyright-protected material and place hardware at the ISP

realise real infrastructures of communication like Wi-Fi and meshed networks and self-made entities for IP broadcast.

Mute: What then are the implications of a 'post-scarcity' system in which the cultural products of immaterial labour are available for free exchange, whilst the cost of living and reproducing oneself rises?

PT: The flow of money and information are immanent to each other. When information is transformed into commodities they become potential allocators of the money you could buy food with. If you are a student you'd rather spend your money on beer and as a parent you spend your money on food rather than paying for CDs or books. If you use alternative circulations like the library, sharing or downloads, your economy becomes richer.

The hacker, the artist or the housewife for that matter, do not live independent from the economic structure of society – on the contrary they are parasites upon existing structures in place within welfare systems, companies and universities. Like all people they are attached to a grey zone where they produce an important surplus value for society that we find more important than most are willing to openly admit. [For a critical discussion of this notion, see Steve Wright's 'Reality Check: are we living in an immaterial world?' in this issue of *Mute*, p.34-45]

Mute: Trackers (and other P2P technologies) are playing a powerful role in the 'economy of attention'. They are becoming important producers of opinion, hype, and desire around new releases from multinationals, as well as facilitating their distribution. Are there ways that Pirate Byran can radicalise this process?

PT: Yes, by bringing in new groups to filesharing. For instance, as in the project 'small pirates' run by PB where the focus is on filesharing for parents and kids, or bringing new content to the trackers as in the project Vidensdeling.nu run by the Danish Pirat Gruppen. I think there is a radical process inherent in the movement, so what is needed is to deepen the understanding of the redistribution of culture. One recent attempt was the book produced by PB about filesharing culture, *Copy Me*. A lot of projects have evolved from the forums at PB. I think it is important to always branch out into different projects so that the process becomes independent from singularities of any kind.

There are always different levels of involvement in a community, some rising and some falling. I think filesharing and open source has a radicalising process

The slogans at the demonstration were: 'Copy me – we will continue to copy everything', 'Don't touch our internet' and 'Welfare begins at 100 Mbit'

attached to it right now because it points to the structural division of information in society. I would say that these links you talk about already exist, the important thing is to make them visible. The best way to do so is to get important files and projects online for filesharing. One of the more recent examples initiated by the sister organisation of the PB in Denmark, Pirat Gruppen, is a project called Vidensdeling.nu. Students are encouraged to digitise and share the expensive books on their reading lists, and in this way use filesharing to create a digital library resource for fellow students, circumventing the costs and control of large publishers. So far, the campaign has resulted in books being shared on The Pirate Bay, while the publishing companies have joined the entertainment industry in their desperate hunt for filesharers. The Pirate Bay can be used by anyone that wants to share files or come up with new models for distribution.

Mute: The asymmetry of access to ownership of communications media is a major factor provoking their seizure and re-distribution. Historically, piracy has arisen at times of enormous economic hegemony (empire), and though formed in opposition to dominant culture frequently plays an economic and geopolitical role in reproducing it. How can the new forms of data piracy support and nourish alternatives and even opposition to dominant economic imperatives?

PT: Overcoming lack of access is not a very important notion in our approach. Not even opposition to dominant forms of culture. Internet piracy is all about desiring-production', and its deepest effects in the long run may well not have so much to do with access, or may go far beyond that notion – just as Walter Benjamin talked about art as the production of desires that cannot yet be satisfied, but will inevitably reach far beyond goals originally impossible to imagine.

Maybe what is most important now is to bypass the urge for solutions, for victory in battles or for compromise and stability. For example, talking about how to 'compensate' copyright holders obscures the truth about the social production of culture, replacing it with the myth of copyright as some kind of 'wage' for artists. On the contrary, trying to keep the 'grey zone' as open and wide as possible, will almost automatically produce better conditions for going beyond prevalent economic imperatives. If nothing else, it will do this by simply curing some of the neurotic sickness of copying-control. But making general statements about different political implications and alternative economic models when talking about piracy and free copying would almost be like accepting copyright's claim to universality.

I think the shift to alternative ways of organising, in more of a rhizomatic manner, is driven by desires and the possibilities of connection. The drive to think, invent and discover alternative processes of production is the affirmative power of life as an experiment in complexity.

URLS
----

http://www.piratbyran.org

http://www.artliberated.org

Palle Torsson <force@chello.se> is a Stockholm based artist, researcher and organiser. He has been a pioneer working with internet, game culture, and intellectual property. He runs the site artliberated.org and works with Pirat Byran, an organisation that fights for the freedom to copy and share media

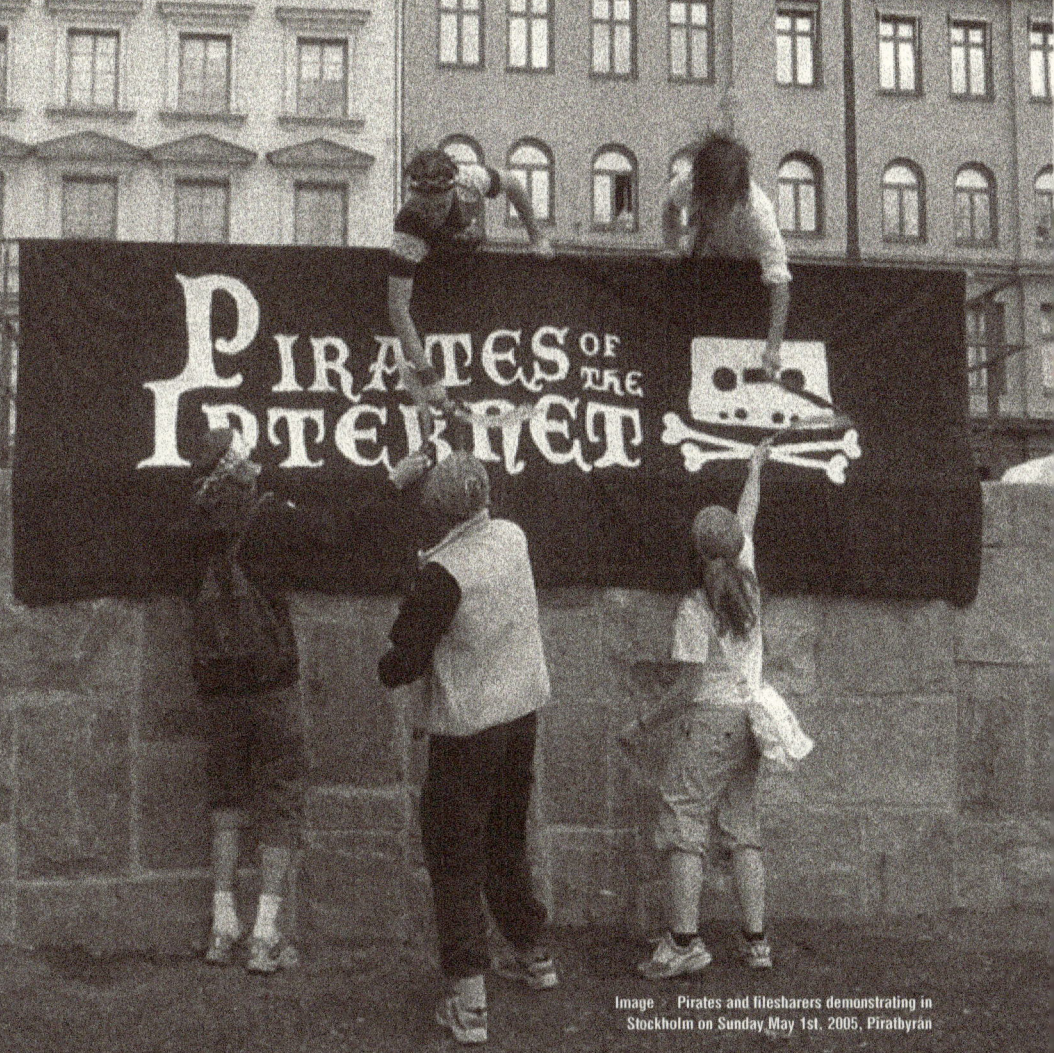

Image > Pirates and filesharers demonstrating in Stockholm on Sunday May 1st, 2005, Piratbyrán

CHARTERS OF LIBERTY IN BLACK FACE AND WHITE FACE: *RACE, SLAVERY AND THE COMMONS*

The Magna Carta is renowned as the 'Charter of Liberty' which inspired modern constitutional safeguards against the power of the State. But its smaller companion, the Charter of the Forest, enshrining the customary rights of the commoners to land and resources, has been overlooked. Cutting between the political struggles of the early 1970s and the 1720s, Peter Linebaugh shows how the struggle against enclosures in the woods of England is inextricably linked with the struggle against slavery in the Atlantic

I am thinking about revolution and constitution, where the former means the overthrow of capitalism and the latter means the ways we re-constitute our governance. Capitalism is the accumulation of commodities, and the production of surplus value by means of unpaid labour. Government concerns the rule of the Many by the Few, a task solved by *divide et impere* and named the Constitution.

The legal cliché is that the American is a written constitution, while the English is unwritten. Yet strictly speaking this is untrue inasmuch as both have stemmed from the Magna Carta of 1215, 790 years ago.

The Norman and Angevin kings afforested as much as a quarter of England, making game reserves, monopolising hydrocarbon energy resources, in zones where

The Charter of the Forest assumes a notion of the 'commons' or a practice of subsistence commoning in the hydrocarbon energy resources of the time

the only law was the king's pleasure. They were crusaders, in world competition with Jews and Arabs for the commerce of the Mediterranean, and to launch such crusades they forced marriages among the barony and took children hostage, pulled teeth of Jewish money lenders, as well as squeezing the serfs and villeins dry. Civil war was the result but cease-fire was obtained with Magna Carta. It revealed the contradictions: between state and church, between monarchs and barons, between them and merchants, between all those three and the commoners who were dependent on forest resources.

Magna Carta has 63 chapters. It is accompanied by a smaller charter, the Charter of the Forest with seventeen chapters. They belong together. They are the two documents printed first in the book of English law for over five centuries. The most esteemed commentators, Edward Coke who influenced the 17th century English Revolution and William Blackstone who influenced the 18th century American Revolution, always treated the two charters as one; the English charters of liberty. We can follow their precedent.

A word about each. The Magna Carta used to be well known and what was most well known in it was chapter 39, because four principles of justice are sometimes derived from it, viz., habeas corpus, trial by jury, prohibition of torture, and due process of law. All of these have been curtailed by the USA Patriot Act. The Charter of the Forest assumes a notion of the 'commons' or a practice of subsistence commoning in the hydrocarbon energy resources of the time. This important presupposition is indicated by technical terms, viz., herbage, assarts, pannage, chiminage, and estovers. Herbage means grazing for cattle; assarts means clearing trees and grubbing stumps for gardening or growing grains; pannage means letting pigs into the woods for mast and nuts; chiminage means no tolls on the roads and paths; estovers means getting wood for fuel, for housing, and for tools and implements.

Now, to express these theoretically we might say that they refer to use-rights rather than to exchange value and thus they refer to particular, concrete labours rather than abstract labour with its universal equivalent in money. From this formulation we might then say they refer to a pre-capitalist mode of production, or we might say they refer to those classes of people whose goal in economic life is the consumption of uses rather than the accumulation of money. In short, they refer to the Many not the Few.

Considering the two charters, some of their provisions concern subsistence and some concern government. Some are negative; they prevent or prohibit arbitrary behavior by armed forces of the king, such as bailiffs, sheriffs, knights and so forth. Others are positive; they provide fuel, travel, food, milk, clothing for commoners. So, like two baskets of law, panniers on the back of a mule, they have trudged down the centuries, sometimes hidden from view or apparently stuck in a slough, at others times requiring a goad to get going again.

There is a third point, the mule can turn around and go the other way. Both charters were committed to disafforestation, or the removal of the king's sole law and the return to conditions prior to the afforestation of the Norman Conquest. Energy resources were to be returned or restored and reparations made for harm done. The King took what did not belong to him; two centuries later he was made to return it. Thus, they reversed two hundred years of history making it, so to speak, go backwards. So much for the self-serving bourgeois doctrine of progress!

The important difference between English and American constitutional development is not that one is unwritten and the other is written. The difference is Africa. American constitutional and revolutionary history depended, first, on taking Indian lands, and, second, on maintenance and expansion of unwaged labour on the plantation where slaves produced surplus value. This is an 18th century problem, as references to the Declaration of Independence and the American Revolution make clear, and as the references of the U.S.A. constitution of 1787 as amended subsequently also makes clear.

In England the protracted struggle to maintain subsistence by access to the commons, or (to express this dynamically) by *making* commons, or commoning, had the unintended consequence of closing England through the repressive response of the Parliamentary Enclosure Acts passed between 1760 and 1830. What was the relationship between, on the one hand, the expropriation from Africans by the slave trade and the resistance to enclosures and, on the other hand, the formation of the working class? This was the problem some of us of 'the Warwick School' set ourselves in the early 1970s. We saw it, at first, as a problem of 'crime'. Then we saw it as a problem of 'custom'. We did not see it as a problem of 'colour', nor did we treat it as a problem of 'capitalism'. Certainly, we failed to see it constitutionally.

To see it as crime was easy enough. George Rudé taught us that revolutionary crowds were criminalised by counter-revolutionaries and their historians. E.J. Hobsbawn taught us that the romanticised criminal, Robin Hood, appears in the transition *into* capitalism but not during the transition *out of* capitalism. Plus were not the great revolutionaries imprisoned, and did not the prisons – Siberia, Kilmainham, Devil's Island, Soledad, Robbin's Island – become seminaries of truth?

What was the relationship between the expropriation from Africans by the slave trade, the resistance to enclosures and the formation of the working class?

We were conscious of colour, because unpaid labour in America depended on it. In 1963 James Baldwin published *The Fire Next Time*, an essay whose wrath anticipated the municipal rebellions of the future but with a title alluding to the rainbow sign.**1** In 1963 the English translation appeared of Franz Fanon's *The Wretched of the Earth* which expressed the hurricane-like energy of the Third World in general and north Africa in particular. It warned against black capitalism. That was also the year of E.P. Thompson's *The Making of the English Working Class* whose version of the working class saved it from Cold War dismissals and whose call to human agency seemed to revive the nerve of change, as it showed the autonomous self-activity of workers in the past in strike, riot, mutiny, and commotion. These American, African, and English voices were anti-capitalist and anti-imperialist.

Between 1963 and 1968 occurred the great municipal rebellions in American ghettoes under the slogan of 'Black power'. How was a revolutionary class analysis to be made? Though we understood Black, we were not yet aware of white. We did not yet understand the DuBois principle of 'the wages of whiteness'.**2**

In 1968 after 'the summer of love' I drove across the country from Columbia University anti-war sit-ins to the Berkeley commune and the bulldozing of People's Park. We stopped in Bloomington, Indiana, in whose rare books library I found a scholarly key to the contradictions besetting the world. It was yet another book by 'anonymous' who in my naiveté I thought was the most frequently mentioned 'author' in the library card catalogue. 'Anonymous' seems to have understood the problem and here was the answer called *The History of the Blacks of Waltham in Hampshire* (1723). I had it photocopied and then protected by some cardboard covers I made and hinged with band-aid tape, which I took with me to England where 'criminality', Black history, and the English working class were going to join, I thought, in a grand revolutionary project. Edward Thompson soon had us formed into a research collective and I gave Edward my treasured copy of *The History of the Blacks* which surely would introduce to England the 'black power' discussions which were rocking the USA. Some years later he returned it, with his marginalia, after it had helped him get started with *Whigs and Hunters* (1975) which was published with *Albion's Fatal Tree* (1975).

He wrote a brilliant book about law and the ruling class, but it was not the book I had dreamed of. It did not lay the axe to the root. I wanted a book about Africans and commoners. I would put forward the fact that the poachers defended commoning, not just by disguising themselves but by disguising themselves *as Negroes,* and they did so at Farnham, near the heart of what became the quintessence of England as Jane Austen so gently wrote about it, or Gilbert White, the ornithologist, so carefully observed it, or William Cobbett, the radical journalist, so persistently fulminated about it.

Round about Farnham timber was wanted for the construction of men-of-war and East Indiamen which stopped in Portsmouth for repairs, or were built there from scratch for the purpose of the globalisation of commodity trade characteristic of the time. Here's how a flashpoint in the episodes of the Waltham Blacks began: 'Mr.

{ 104 }

Image   Anja Kirschner

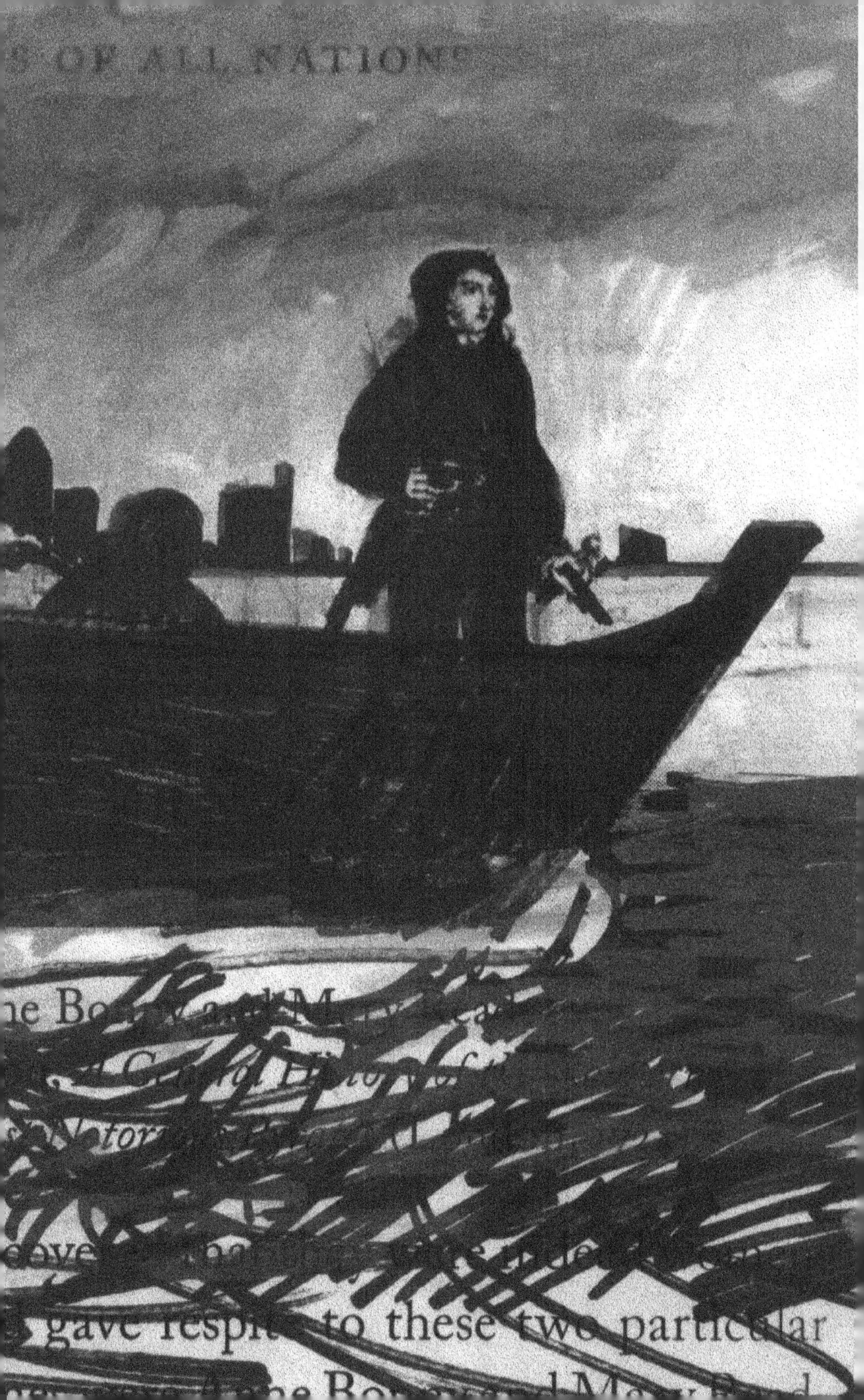
OF ALL NATIONS

Wingfield who has a fine Parcel of growing Timber on his Estate near Farnham fell'd Part of it: The poor People were admitted (as is customary) to pick up the small Wood; but some abusing the Liberty given, carry'd off what was not allow'd, which that Gentleman resented; and, as an Example to others, made several pay for it. Upon which, the Blacks summon'd the Myrmidons, stripp'd the Bark off several of the standing Trees, and notch'd the Bodies of others, thereby to prevent their Growth; and left a Note on one of the maim'd Trees, to inform the Gentleman, that this was their first Visit; and that if he did not return the Money receiv'd for Damage, he must expect a second from ... the Blacks.' This is not exactly tree-hugging or Indian chipko, though it did have warrant among local antiquarians in the nineteenth century who searched for a charter of such commoning. The leader of the Blacks and '15 of his Sooty Tribe appear'd, some in Coats made of Deer-Skins, others with Fur Caps, &c. all well armed and mounted: There were likewise at least 300 People assembled to see the *Black Chief* and his *Sham* Negroes....'

Charles Withers, Surveyor-General of Woods, observed in 1729 'that the country people everywhere think they have a sort of right to the wood & timber in the forests, and whether the notion may have been delivered down to them by tradition, from the times these forests were declared to be such by the Crown, when there were great struggles and contests about them, he is not able to determine.' The Waltham Blacks, they said, 'had no other design but to do justice, and to see that the Rich did not insult or oppress the poor.' They were assured that the chase was 'originally design'd to feed Cattle, and not to fatten deer for the clergy, &c.' The central common right was pasture, 'common of herbage' as the Forest Charter says. Keeping a cow was possible on two acres, and less in a forest or fen. Half the villagers of England were entitled to common grazing. As late as the 18th century 'all or most householders in forest, fen, and some heathland parishes enjoyed the right to pasture cows or sheep.'3 So, the Waltham Blacks were class conscious. There was also an awareness at the time that the keeping of a cow, essential to the material constitution of the country, was backed up by charter.

Timothy Nourse denounced commoners at the beginning of the century. They were 'rough and savage in their Dispositions.' They held 'leveling Principles.' They were 'insolent and tumultuous' and 'refractory to Government.'4 In September 1723 Richard Norton, the Warden of the Forest of Bere, wished to 'put an end to these arabs and banditti.' The commoner belonged to a 'sordid race.' The commoner was compared to the Indian, to the savage, to the buccaneer, and to the Arab.

The 'Blacks' defended the customs of the commoners; the commoners were both criminalised and racialised in the discourse of the enclosers, the privatisers, and the big

the poachers defended commoning, not just by disguising themselves but by disguising themselves as *Negroes*

wigs. There was even the suggestion that attacking them was a sort of crusade. The Waltham Black Act of 1722 thus became, among other things, a means of drawing a colour line and criminalising common right.**5**

We can put forward as evidence what was neglected in Thompson, the fact of the African slave trade. Blacking, wrote the anonymous historian in that treasured pamphlet history, commenced 'about the times of general confusion, when the late pernicious schemes of the South Sea Company boure all things down before them, and laid waste what the industry and good husbandry of families had gather'd together.'**6** The South Sea Company was a slave trading company, formed a few years earlier, to take advantage of the *asiento* or licence to trade to Spanish America. On September 11, 1713, Royal African Company congratulated itself on obtaining 'such advantageous terms, as never were before granted to the people who undertook the furnishing of negroes to the Spanish West Indies.' The crisis of the commons began as a financial crisis which itself arose from slaving.

The South Sea Bubble was the wreck of a kind of capitalist commoning. Thirty years earlier, this new form of commoning had been produced through developments within English constitutional governance. During the 1690s sovereign legal authority (King-in-Parliament) united with the financial form of value resulting in the Bank of England, Lloyd's Insurance Company, the Coinage Act, &c. Money and other financial instruments liquefied the clumsy, cumbersome form of wealth as private property which was presented as use values in warehouses, docks, ships, shops, etc., and moreover placed it directly under fiscal state command. The creation of monetary liquidity permitted the distribution of surplus value as investment in various commercial and industrial enterprises according to the needs of capital as a whole without regard to rates of exploitation in individual enterprises. Investment and speculation appeared insubstantial, disembodied, atmospheric or gaseous. The South Sea 'bubble' popped owing to cupidity which seemed infinite and to anonymous Atlantic obstacles, namely, resistance, recalcitrance, and revolt.

The decade between 1716 and 1726 was the golden age of piracy, Marcus Rediker informs us.**7** The significance of piracy during these years was twofold – it was multiracial and it was against the slave trade. They blockaded ports, disrupted the sea lanes. The pirate ship 'might be considered a multiracial maroon community.' Hundreds were African. Sixty of Blackbeard's crew of a hundred were black. Rediker quotes the Negro of Deptford who in 1721 led 'a Mutiny that we had too many Officers, and that work was too hard, and what not.' They also prevented the slave trade from growing. This was the complaint of Humphrey Morice, MP, Governor of the Bank of England, owner of a small fleet of slavers, who led the petitioning to Parliament and who suffered severe losses in 1719, the year that serious blacking commenced. A naval squadron was sent to west Africa. Four hundred and eighteen pirates were hanged. The conjuncture of apparently very distant forces, struggle for

The South Sea 'bubble' popped owing to infinite cupidity and anonymous Atlantic obstacles, namely, resistance, recalcitrance, and revolt

common rights and the Atlantic slave trade, in fact met in intimate proximity.

Daniel Defoe, the most prolific prose writer in the English language, was preoccupied with the issues of Atlantic labour power. Coincidentally, his writing transpired during the privatisation of the printed word by means of Queen Anne's Copyright Act. He precisely combined the intimate conjunction of opposites with a trans-Atlantic background. *Robinson Crusoe, Mariner* was published in 1719. The book dramatises the labour theory of value, glories in the intricacies of the division of labour, and puts the European foot (Crusoe) on the African neck (Friday). Alexander Selkirk, the actual person who was the prototype of *Robinson Crusoe,* died in February 1721 as a sailor in a naval squadron that was sent to west Africa to extirpate the piracy interrupting the slave trade. *The Adventures and Misadventures of Moll Flanders,* published in 1722 treats the issues of criminalisation of the commons and large scale cooperative labour. Upward social mobility was not accomplished by 'affirmative action' but negative criminality, as Moll Flanders hooked up with highwaymen on the first step of the ladder of success and whose final rung she at last attained – a Virginia tobacco plantation – so she too could put the boot to the African enslaved.

These are the classic fictional disquisitions on subsistence, survival, and surplus in that era of off-shore and homeland plunder; they also present heroic prototypes of the 'white' worker. Indeed, these novels coincided almost to the year with 'the invention of the white race,' to give the title of Ted Allen's compelling thesis.[8] A buffer stratum was to be created by offering material advantages to white proletarians to the lasting detriment of black proletarians. When and how did the 'wages of whiteness' originate? The first date DuBois gives in the protracted process is 1723 when laws were passed in Virginia making Africans and Anglo-Africans slaves forever. The bonded people objected in 1723 to the Bishop of London and the King 'and the rest of the Rullers.' 'Releese us out of this Cruell Bondegg' they cried. In the same year Richard West, the Attorney General, objected to the same law, 'I cannot see why one freeman should be used worse than another, merely upon account of his complexion....' But the Governor of Virginia understood the necessity of 'a perpetual Brand' – skin colour, or the phenotype, which marked the person as surely as the burnt flesh caused by the golden brands used by the South Sea Company. In this way, Ted Allen tells us, a 'monstrous social mutation' occurred, namely, that stratum within the American class structure which derives its hopes, security, and welfare from white skin privilege. It has been essential to the constitution of American class relations ever since.

This was not known to Thompson. The experience within England (though not Ireland) was different, where the policing of the wage relationship, or the exploitation of the Many by the Few, did not depend upon the colour line, and where therefore it was unnecessary to constitute that structure of white supremacy. Thompson wrote the famous 'rule of law' coda to *Whigs and Hunters*. 'As the last imperial illusions of the twentieth century fade, so preoccupation with the history and culture of a small island off the coast of Europe becomes open to the charge of narcissism. The culture of constitutionalism which flowered here, under favoured conditions, is an episode too exceptional to carry any universal significance.' Yet, even smaller than England was the island where Robinson Crusoe met Friday and that story spread world-wide.

The colonists of the north American mainland, even at the time of *Robinson Crusoe* (1719), the Waltham Black Act (1722), and the South Sea Bubble (1722), had begun to graft some of that English constitutionalism to their own purposes. For example, *The New-England Courant* in its summer issue of 1722 sought to be rectify the stupidity of the colonists by quoting chapter 39 of Magna Carta and commented, 'No Freeman shall be taken, &c. These words deserve to be written in letters of gold, and I have often wondred that they are not inscribed in Capitals in all our Courts of Judicature, Town-halls, and most publick edifices; they being essential to our English Freedom and Liberties...' 'No man ought to be put from his Livelyhood without answer' rings hollow to the unemployed, or to the Indians who were proclaimed rebels in the same newspaper for attacking fifteen commercial vessels intruding on their fishing grounds and whose women and children were taken in captivity to Dunstable. 'No man can be exiled or banished out of his native country' is hypocrisy to the men and women and children from the west coast of Africa enslaved in America. *The New England Courant*'s sole advertisement reads 'A likely Negro Woman to be sold by Mr. *Thomas Selby* at the Crown Coffee-House, the lower end of Kingstreet.'

Thompson, however, did not accept a 'South Sea' or Atlantic perspective, much less a planetary one in his references to constitutionalism. He reversed himself, moving from a mood of postcolonial narcissism to one of praise for the English ruling class as a whole: '... the inhibitions upon power imposed by laws seem to me a legacy as substantial as any handed down from the struggles of the seventeenth century to the eighteenth, and a true and important cultural achievement of the agrarian and mercantile bourgeoisie, and of their supporting yeomen and artisans.' And when Thompson writes of the culture of constitutionalism, why does he exclude the charters of liberty?

Dorothy Thompson, many years later, attributed this coda to heated arguments that she had with her husband and co-worker, Edward, arguing that 'he was leaning too far in the direction taken by some of the contributors to *Albion's Fatal Tree* in

In 1774 the former African-American slave, Olaudah Equiano, put on white face in London in order to obtain a warrant of habeas corpus

dismissing the law simply as an instrument of class power.'9 The context of the discussions about these books took place in 1970 and 1971; when for instance Howard Zinn in November 1970 said 'The Problem is Civil Disobedience', and he ran down the law, how the bill of rights is publicised but not enforced, how the property laws are enforced but not publicised. He showed how decorum and propriety fool us and cause us to revere the law. He reminded us that often we have to go outside the legal framework – the Civil War, the Union drives, the American Revolution. He said 'people in all countries need the spirit of disobedience to the state....' The American and the English experiences were different. The Attica revolt was in September 1971, and the trial of the Mangrove Nine was finished in 1971. Internment without trial was introduced in 1971, and 'Bloody Sunday' was in January 1972. These events of state terrorism were not yet answered by similar violence of those taking an anti-imperialist stand. Furthermore, they still seemed part of an ancient constitution in which 'race' played trumps.

Our books were not published until 1975. During the interval the world changed direction. The PLO assassinated Israeli athletes at the Munich Olympics. The IRA brought the war to England. The Guildford pub bombing of October 1974 left five dead, a month later the Birmingham pub bombing killed twenty-one. While the political climate became more violent, the intellectual climate became more academic, more legalistic, more obscure. Critical Legal Studies (formed in 1977) stuck to the high theory of Frankfurt School and French post-structuralism, obtusely reluctant to engage English social history, or to raise the constitutional issues of race or the commons.

There is a vast amount of English social history since 1975 (and before) recording the importance of customary rights to common forest resources. Moreover, that story is now clearly understood to have happened all over the world. J.M. Neeson produced a great book about the commons from earlier discussions concerning custom. Called *Commoners*, it showed that subsistence use-rights remained a material basis of many English agrarian workers. Meanwhile, others of us adduced the evidence that the wage relation arose from the process of criminalisation and the process of criminalisation arose from custom. The irrationality of the wage concealed the unpaid labour. But could these *aperçus* attain constitutional importance or were they destined to dismissal as un-theorised ditty?

> The law locks up the man or woman
> Who steals the goose from off the common
> But lets the greater villain loose
> Who steals the common from the goose

The violence and the terror, 'the military option' as the Italian Red Brigades put it, made it harder to see the Charters, or the commons, as anything other than a wild goose chase. Looking back now we can see that the issue was not the rule of law against terrorism: the issue was the preservation of commoning against new enclosures.

We could use some theory of the kind that transformed Magna Carta for the Levellers, of the kind that transformed Magna Carta for the abolitionists. In 1774 the former African-American slave, Olaudah Equiano, put on white face in London in order to obtain a warrant of habeas corpus. This is among the first actions by which Magna Carta was appropriated for the trans-Atlantic movement to abolish slavery. In the same year Granville Sharp wrote 'The wisdom of ages has made [Magna Carta] venerable, and stamped it with an authority equal to the Constitution itself, of which it is, in reality, a most essential and fundamental part; so that any attempt to repeal it would be treason to the State! This glorious Charter must, therefore, ever continue unrepealed: and even the articles which seem at present useless, must ever remain in force.'**10** Granville Sharpe used the charters against slavery, racial and otherwise, but, despite an obsession with the gothic frankpledge, he did not take his stand with the commons, unlike Thomas Spence or Gracchus Babeuf. Similarly with Frederick Douglass who said in 1854, 'Let the engine of the Magna Carta beat against the Jericho walls of Slavery, and no seven days blowing of ram's horns would be necessary,' a reference to the jubilee which, while emancipating slaves, also restored the commons.

Edward Thompson failed to mention Magna Carta and more strategically he omitted the Charter of the Forest. There was an opportunity to link the constitution to the commons at that point in time, Walpole 1720-1723, when some English and African commoners could be found together on the seven seas and in the wild wood. The moment passed: privatisation and slavery advanced together. We hear Blackstone crow as he defined private property as 'that sole and despotic common which one man claims and exercises over the external things of the world, in total exclusion of the right of any other individual in the universe.' (He admitted in his *Commentaries* that there are elements such as light, air, and water which 'must still unavoidably remain in common.')

Today, the commons comes back to us from the South! Subcommandante Marcos provided the voice of the Zapatistas and the indigenous people of Chiapas calling for the return of Article 27 and the *ejidos*, or common land, while reminding us of the Magna Carta. As the Many demand water, energy, and wherewithal against the surplus value hogged by the Few, we must reprise those moments when the act of constitution showed not racist *divide et impere* but that old, old friend of all, the commons. This enterprise calls for our contemporary appropriations of *both* of the Charters of Liberty. ⚐

FOOTNOTES

1 The title alludes to a slave song:
'God gave Noah the rainbow sign,
No more water, the fire next time'. Editor's note.

2 David Roediger, *The Wages of Whiteness: Race and the
Making of the American Working Class* (Verso: New York,
1991). In the preparation of this essay I thank David Roediger
and his colleagues at the University of Illinois, Champaign-
Urbana

3 J.M. Neeson, *Commoners: Common Right, Enclosure, and
Social Change in England, 1700-1820* (Cambridge, 1993), p. 317

4 Timothy Nourse, *Campania Foelix, Or a Discourse of the
Benefits and Improvements of Husbandry* (1700), pp. 15-16

5 'The Black Act was instituted in 1723... in response to the
Waltham deer poachers. It made it a felony (that is, a
hanging offence) to appear armed in a park or warren, or to
hunt or steal deer, with the face blackened or disguised...',
http://en.wikipedia.org/wiki/Black_Act

6 *The History of the Blacks of Waltham in Hampshire*,
Anonymous, (1723)

7 Marcus Rediker, *Villains of All Nations: Atlantic Pirates in
the Golden Age* (Beacon Press: Boston, 2004)

8 Ted Allen, *The Invention of the White Race, volume two,
The Origin of Racial Oppression in Anglo-America* (Verso,
1997)

9 Daniel H. Cole, '"An Unqualified Human Good": E.P.
Thompson and the Rule of Law'
http://papers.ssrn.com/sol3/papers.cfm?abstract_id=169264

10 *A Declaration of the People's Natural Right to a Share in
the Legislature* (1774), pp. 202-3

Peter Linebaugh <plineba@yahoo.com> teaches history at
the University of Toledo in Ohio where he is also writing a
book on the Charters of Liberty

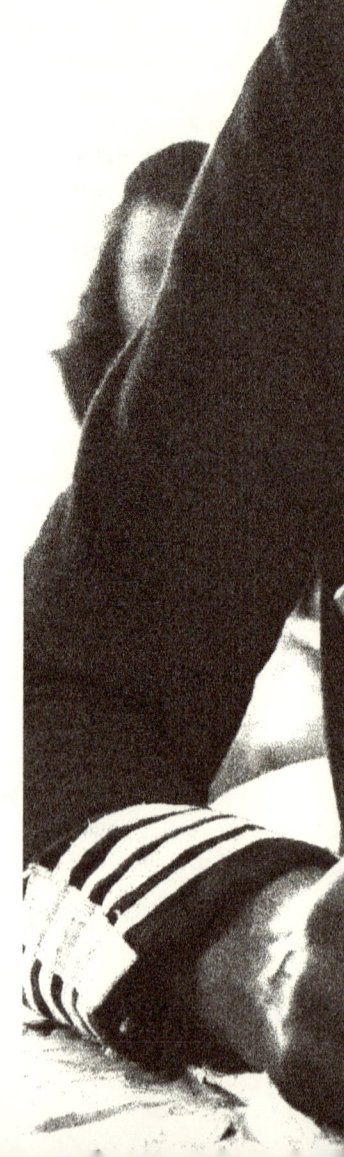

Film still >> from *Polly II*, Anja Kirschner
Photograph: Alessandra Chila

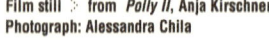

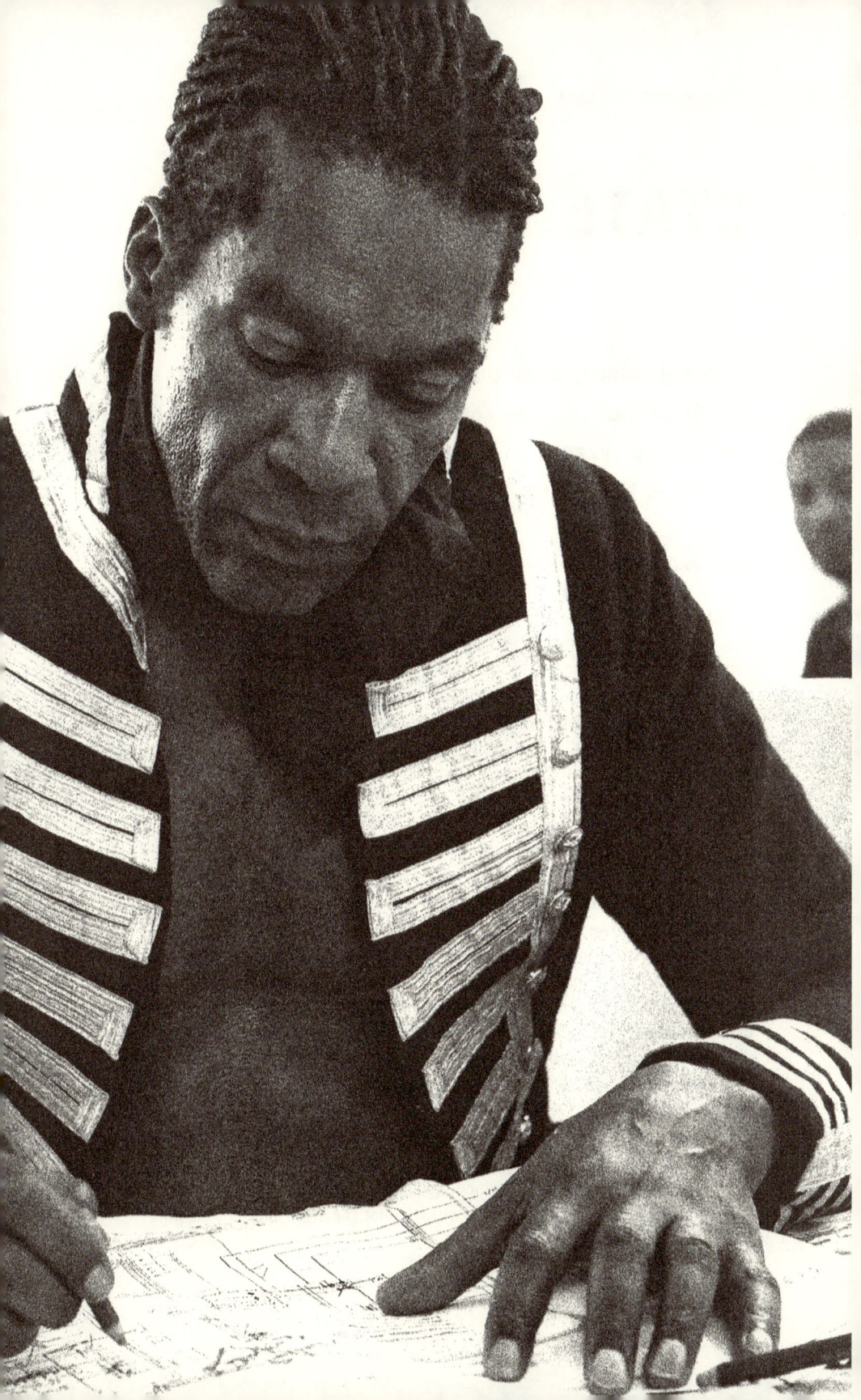

STATE WIDE SHUT

A recent report, *Wide Open*, by the think tank Demos takes the metaphor of open source and runs with it – right into the closed kernel of the modern state. Gregor Claude examines the debris

What would an open source government look like? The question is being asked not, as you might think, by wild-eyed, fast-coding techno-anarchists intent on squatting the geopolitical noosphere, but in the pragmatically modernising world of New Labour think-tankery. A new report, *Wide Open: Open Source Methods and their Future Potential*, was published this April by the British think tank Demos and co-authored by Downing Street insiders Geoff Mulgan and Tom Steinberg. It explores the lessons, methods, and success stories of open source, and offers suggestions about how they might be applied to governing people rather than code. But can you really open up the state to distributed tinkering, and if so, what would that mean? I can think of a few things that would make my list but I don't think that's what they have in mind: debugging the police, rebooting the kernel panic on terror, compiling a few decent hospitals...

Open source has firmly established its role in non-commercial software production, but it has also generated a buzz about its wider social and political applications for some time now. Radical writers and activists were the first to get excited about it, but now it has also found an important niche in the business plans of commercial giants like IBM and Sun Microsystems. And predictably, in tandem, open source software is also appearing on the to-do lists of official political bodies, whether states or NGOs, who are wary of the strategic implications of being locked into a relationship with Microsoft.

But Mulgan and Steinberg want to think beyond simply installing Linux on the computers of Whitehall. Admirably, they know enough about computers to recognise the limits of applying the metaphor of open source to anything other than software. Source code is the human-readable computer code which is compiled into the machine-readable software that computers actually run. The state may sometimes have a newspeak translation problem, but it is not the same as this one. What

Mulgan and Steinberg really want to think about is how a less than popular state can connect with what it sees as apathetic populations and engage their energies. They list the aspects of open source that they feel may prove particularly valuable, including:

> transparency
> vetting of participants only after they've got involved
> low cost and ease of engagement
> a legal structure and enforcement mechanism
> leadership
> common standards
> peer review and feedback loops
> a shared conception of goals
> incrementalist – small players can still make useful contributions
> powerful non-monetary incentives

Much of this reads like the virtues of a dependable community social club. But above all, the report and its recommendations is primarily about open source as metaphor for a new organisational model, one which turns away from the hierarchical and the bureaucratic in favour of the decentralised network.

This is in some ways quite a departure – hierarchy and bureaucracy has been the form of the modern state throughout its existence. Rulers and their thinkers have conceived of the state as a 'body politic', with the sovereign as the controlling head and the rest of us as subordinate organs, for almost as long as there have been states. The metaphor is found in the Hindu Vedas and the Mahabharata, was given a particularly influential elaboration in Plato's *Republic*, and it has become more or less common sense in the era of the modern state. It is a metaphor extended beyond the state to society at large by the discipline of Sociology – Durkheim considered his new science as opening up the possibility for a kind of medical practice capable of treating the pathologies of the modern social body when its 'organic solidarity' was threatened. Max Weber, on the other hand, despaired that the all-pervasive organisational practice of bureaucracy was so ruthlessly efficient that, once entrenched, nothing could displace it, and humanity faced an ever-more organised, bureaucratised and hierarchical future.

Is it really possible that the British State might break with this organisational orthodoxy? Could New Labour have discovered (and modernised, of course) the philosophical disorganisationalists Deleuze and Guattari? In their book *Thousand Plateaus*, their concept of the body without organs is, in its most basic sense, an argument against rigid, bureaucratic organisation. Against the organised body, with its strictly delimited division of labour between its specialised organs, its static fixity

So what would the state, the head and chief organiser of the body politic, want with a headless rhizome?

of functions, and its hierarchical system of control. The body without organs is dynamic, flowing, collective and... open. It is not anti-order, but its order is 'rhizomatic', like a decentralised network, rather than 'arborescent', branching like a tree from a single source. To organise is to segment a dynamic flow of energies into discrete containable units, and above all, to coordinate those units with a single command structure. So what would the state, the head and chief organiser of the body politic, want with a headless rhizome?

Mulgan and Steinberg's encouragements centre on using open source methods as a new organisational model for re-thinking (at least to some extent) the relationship between state and society. Open source methods of organisation appear to them to offer the possibility of blurring the boundaries between the state and the public. One of the claims made for open source organisation in software is that it breaks down the boundaries of one of the basic units of economic production, the firm. Production is no longer something that takes place in a particular time (the working day) and place (the factory or office, or even something that happens among a tightly defined group (employees). Rather, creativity and production is something that is at least as likely to happen outside the boundaries of the firm. What then becomes important is not to try to recapture this creativity inside the boundaries of the firm, but to allow some of the boundaries of the firm to dissolve, and to merely coordinate the flows of creativity in such a way that the porous firm can profit from it.

Whether or not open source coordination can be effectively deployed by the state is an open question. Mulgan and Steinberg do put forward several notable, if low-key suggestions. What they call 'pre-legislative scrutiny' appears to amount to online focus groups to help legislators research public opinion about pending legislative proposals. In local government the scope suggested is even bolder: with these 'very local rules', they write, 'there is no reason why they could not be opened up to popular ownership'. Sure, why not, but it does leave you thinking that after all that optimistic open talk, tossing us local by-laws for our popular ownership is a pretty paltry offering. 'Free the source code to a few parking lots and business licences!' – not sure quite who that rallying cry is directed towards. The voluntarist minorities who are bothered about parking and zoning restrictions are presumably already well known at their town halls and council meetings. These are obviously not suggestions for dissolving the boundaries of the various organs of state or re-thinking the principle of bureaucratic hierarchy. Rather these are suggestions about how an existing bureaucratic hierarchy can deploy a strategy of porosity and openness to extend itself into the 'community', and with them comes a strong resonance with other New Labour community building projects.

In the final days of the dotcom bubble, virtual reality pioneer Jaron Lanier noted sceptically that as a computer scientist, people were always telling him that his field was the 'central metaphor of everything'. Open source has for many become yet another central metaphor of everything, and it's hard not to be a little cautious. There is clearly an appetite for experimentation here, but it is the appetite of the New Labour rootless moderniser who, having lost any real political constituency years ago, will try anything to reach out and touch The Community. Whether it succeeds in anything more ambitious than a suggestion box on Downing Street's website is another question.

URLS
----
http://www.demos.co.uk/catalogue/wideopen/

Gregor Claude <gregor@zoom.co.uk> is a lecturer at the Centre for Cultural Studies, Goldsmiths College

This compilation of conference proceedings (6-8 January 2005, Delhi) links a wide spectrum of political, social and cultural issues embedded in "the property question". It deconstructs the capital-driven processes of enclosure in the contexts of software, file-sharing, patents, biopiracy, Indigenous knowledge, cyber art, virtual exchange, literary history, theology and law, among others.

Varied voices explore new paradigms of practice in relation to the global intellectual property regime, its enforcement as well as its violation and subversion by a compelling array of resilient figures. These include the hacker, the pirate, the solitary "genius", the reformer, the artist, the prisoner, the heretic, the thief, the "transformative" author, the theorist, the migrant, the vendor, the critic, the aesthete, the scribe, the citizen, the tenant, the worker, the chairman, the rebel, the coder, the squatter, the inventor, the farmer, the smuggler, the spectator, the judge...

This detailed account describes the radical contemporary shifts in the production, distribution and consumption of cultural materials through the networks of digital media. It complicates the meaning of "community", and narrates how technology continues to enable an unprecedented levelling of exclusionary hierarchies and hegemonies all over the world.

Available for free download at www.sarai.net/events/ip_conf/ip_conf.htm
Paperback, 170 pp, Euro 10, US$ 10

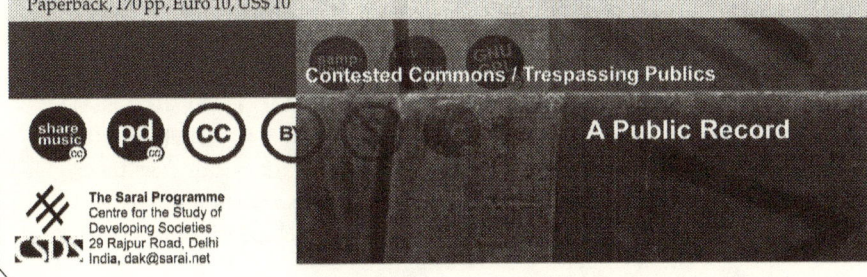

Contested Commons / Trespassing Publics

A Public Record

share music | pd | cc | BY

The Sarai Programme
Centre for the Study of
Developing Societies
29 Rajpur Road, Delhi
India, dak@sarai.net

GENDER DIMENSIONS OF FLOSS DEVELOPMENT

The FLOSS ideal of equality, inclusivity and freeness is sadly let down by the gender imbalance of its participants, with women comprising just over 1 percent of FLOSS developers. Yuwei Lin analyses the causes of the gender digital divide and suggests a way to help close it

INTRODUCTION

Software is at the heart of the development of information communication technologies (ICTs). In an ICT based society, it is increasingly important that software is designed to meet the requirements of diverse users. To do so, several software processes have been proposed to update the traditional ones. Methods such as Participatory Design (PD), agile computing, User-Centred Design (UCD), and eXtreme Programming (XP).**1** These methodologies, though different, have a common goal of making software products more friendly and more diverse for various types of end users. The development mode of Free/Libre Open Source Software (FLOSS) is one of the most common and successful examples of this aim.

FLOSS has become a prominent phenomenon in ICT field and the wider public domain in the past years. Its success has also attracted researchers from different disciplines to analyse its unconventional innovation approach. But according to a FLOSS survey on FLOSS developers in 2002, 'women do not play a role in [FLOSS] development; only 1.1% of the FLOSS sample is female.**2** In the mainstream research on the FLOSS community, many researchers also overlook the diversity of the members, and presume a stereotyped male dominated 'hacker community'. Moreover, the issue of gender inequality is often ignored and/or muted, in the pile of FLOSS studies. Not only are female programmers often rejected ex/implicitly from the software labour market, but also the needs of female users are not respected and consulted.**3** This feature is opposite to the ideal world of FLOSS where all users are

Only 1.1 percent of the FLOSS sample is female

treated equally and embraced. Compared with the abundant literature on the processes of FLOSS development, the gender problem is marginalised. While many researchers endeavour to understand the process and structure of FLOSS related organisations and management, few find a gender biased situation problematic. In short, women are almost invisible in current FLOSS related literature and most policies advocating FLOSS development are gender blind.

Thus, this essay highlights the need for increased action to address imbalances between women's and men's access to and participation in FLOSS development in cultural (e.g. chauvinistic and/or gender biased language in discussions on mailing lists or in documentation), economic (e.g. unequal salary levels for women and men), political (e.g. male dominated advocacy environments) and technical (e.g. gender inbalance amongst students in technical tutorials) spheres. But on the other hand, it also emphasises the powerful potential of FLOSS as a vehicle for advancing gender equality in software expertise. FLOSS helps transfer software engineering knowledge and experience through the distribution of source code and binary code almost without limit. Many free software licences such as the General Public Licence (GPL) also facilitate the flow of information and knowledge. In other words, if appropriately harnessed, FLOSS stands to meaningfully contribute to and reinforce the advancement of effective, more expedient solutions to bridging the gender digital divide. This article also points out that while women in advanced countries have a better chance of upgrading their ICT skills and knowledge through participating in FLOSS development, the opportunity is less available for women in the developing world. It is worth noting that though the gender issues raised in this essay are widespread, they should not be considered as universal. Regional specificities affecting gender roles within the software industry should be taken into account.**4**

GENDER PROBLEMS IN THE SOFTWARE INDUSTRY

To a degree, the gender problems in FLOSS development can be seen as an extension of the ongoing gender issues in new tech service and software industries.**5** These long term problems mainly include low level work content, unequal pay, emotional distress from discrimination and prejudice, physical ache from the long working hour in front of the computer, division of labour within the home (child rearing), essentialist notions of women's roles, sexism, informal networks, prejudice, lack of role models and support, and 'glass ceilings'. Generally speaking, women within the software industry have to work harder than men in order to get the same respect and conquer the glass ceiling problem in this patriarchal world.**6**

Many studies have undermined the stereotyped presumption of a biological sex difference between men and women causing women to be less interested in scientific and technological fields.**7** Instead, there is significant evidence that that school curriculum and methods of teaching technology in school should be adjusted to bridge the gender gap**8** through educational means, such as encouraging women to pursue higher education or jobs in scientific and technological areas, and governmental policies to support and promote women in ICT.

The software industry has perceived these problems and tried to solve them. For instance, HP, Sun, Xerox and Compaq have sponsored the Institute for Women and Technology (IWT)**9** and other universities in a US wide program to bridge the gender gap in technology and support the development of technology products focused on women's interests and needs. Most of the software companies now also provide a series of women friendly policies, including extended maternity and paternity leave, accommodation for emergency leave, and superior benefits, in order to cover childcare and family accommodation. Unfortunately, according to observers, motherhood is still seen as a liability for women's advancement, and the pay of women continues to suffer after having children.**10** The software industry is socially constructed - men's superiority over women and an essentialist gender division of work are continuously reiterated.**11**

TOWARDS A FEMINIST ANALYSIS OF GENDER ISSUES IN FLOSS DEVELOPMENT

Although FLOSS has dramatically changed the way software is produced, distributed, supported, and used, and has a visible social impact enabling richer digital inclusivity, most of the gender problems existing in the software industry have been duplicated in the FLOSS field.

The methodological concepts 'social world' and 'system' can help in understanding FLOSS development.**12** A FLOSS social world is different from what Sherry Turkle described when she stated that 'computer systems [mainly proprietary] represent a closed, controllable microworld - which appeals to more men than women'.**13** It requires a holistic perspective to capture the complexity and dynamics within and across the (FLOSS) social world. While its heterogeneity and contingency has not yet been fully explored, analysis from a feminist perspective is almost absent. Little attention has been paid to internal differences and to the private domain which connects to the system of FLOSS innovation. However, this methodological lack has not stopped us from observing the gender problems within the field. Instead, in the context of FLOSS development, some gender problems in ICT become even more apparent.

For example, most FLOSS graphic interfaces appear less advanced. The mainly text based nature of FLOSS is so predominant that women, who usually have few coding experiences, are less familiar with its operation. Instead of stemming from some biological sex difference, the phenomenon suggests a lingering deficiency of women's

Most of the gender problems in the software industry have been duplicated in the **FLOSS** field

IT education and women-unfriendly products and tools.

Additionally, in a world of volunteers, we clearly see that, as in all media, both men, and a competitive world view are dominant in FLOSS. Many women participating in FLOSS development are invisible; their labour in fields such as NGOs that help implement and promote FLOSS documentation, translation, book editing, teaching and tutoring (e.g. E-Riders) is less visible than it is in the male dominated field of coding work.**14**

Indeed, in light of Okin's argument, I would like to suggest that FLOSS advocates have not adequately addressed this critique of gender equality.**15** They tend to treat the FLOSS community as a monolithic culture and pay more attention to differences between groups than to differences within them. They are so eager to unite the voices around the fight for freedom of information that they give little or no recognition to the fact that FLOSS groups, 'like the societies in which they exist (though to a greater or lesser extent), are themselves *gendered*, with substantial differences of power and advantage between men and women.'**16** Apart from that, FLOSS advocates often do not take the private sphere into account when proposing an alternative agenda for a knowledge based society, which is often articulated as the 'public domain'. This relativisation of the private sphere is unwise in that it 'neglect[s] both the different roles that groups require of their members and the context in which persons' senses of themselves and their capacities are first formed *and* in which culture is first transmitted - the realm of domestic or family life.'**17** In other words, if a more liberal and democratised information society were to be established, as the FLOSS movement intends, domestic arrangements need to be taken into consideration. 'Home is, after all, where much of culture is practiced, preserved, and transmitted to the young.'**18**

A number of key dilemmas that hinder women's participation in FLOSS development can be summarised thus:

1) Strong long-hour coding culture
In terms of women's relation to and experience of FLOSS, it is observed that women are found mostly taking trainee positions that follow regular nine-to-five working hours, rather than a less stable coding job. This often is due to the fact that women need to take care of the housework and require steadier working hours. A successful FLOSS project requires volunteers to commit to it progressively but women usually have less spare time and energy to donate than men. This way of working makes it very difficult for women to succeed in the business. It must be incredibly hard for women with children to navigate the hours. If men could share the child-rearing

more equally, it would allow women more time to take on the consuming role of programming or leading a FLOSS project.

2) A lack of 'mentors' and role models

It is true that there is a very low percentage of female participants in the FLOSS social world. However, we should not overlook the importance and possible future of outstanding female figures in the FLOSS field such as Allison Randal and Amaya to name two who are already making a difference.**19** It is difficult to make the majority of male peers respect these female figures. For instance, I have observed that when Randal spoke at the Italian Code Jam 2004, she acted, and also was treated, as more of an assistant to Larry Wall rather than an outstanding programmer who should be granted the respect of her male peers. I am not suggesting that men all look down on women, but it is more difficult for women to be assertive in front of a predominantly male audience.**20** The whole way the world is constructed means there are simply men at every level, which makes it really hard for women to get their foot in the door. A way of overcoming this is to establish more female luminaries in the IT world. While few actually know that Ms. Ada Byron was the first programmer in the world, how can we expect people to recognise women's ability?

3) Discriminating languages on/offline

There is still a strong 'chauvinistic mentality', extended from the society we live in to the FLOSS social world. As the barrier to accessing FLOSS references is relatively low compared with other proprietary software projects, there should be fewer problems for participants regardless of gender, class, ethnicity and religion. However, many female FLOSS developers have complained of the extremely unfriendly atmosphere within the social world, online (e.g. mailing lists, IRCs) and/or offline (e.g. documentation). For instance, in reference to prospective readers, existing FLOSS documentation usually uses the pronoun 'he' rather than 'she' or 'they'. This kind of gender-biased word use subtly excludes women from participating in the FLOSS development. While the online languages are in a direct way full of men's jargon, reading the documentation offline does not make a female developer/user feel more included in the field.

4) A gendered text based environment

A text based coding environment somehow reinforces the gendering of ICT. In saying so, I am not suggesting that women are less equipped for coding in a text based environment; instead, I would like to argue that such a coding environment symbolises its remoteness and the difficulty of establishing subjectivity within a male dominated coding culture.

The difference between text based and graphic environments hinges on the issue of ability to recall the keystrokes and commands. Coding in a text based

If appropriately har-nessed, FLOSS stands to meaningfully contribute to effective, expedient solutions to bridging the gender digital divide

environment is useful for those who use tools so regularly that they can easily recall the commands. Graphic environments help present commands in visual forms for users who would otherwise have to look them up. It is often said that coding environments are just a matter of taste and separate from gender or other social factors. However, if this is only a matter of preference, why is there such a prevalent impression, if not stereotype, that being able to code in a text based environment shows greater computer literacy? Doesn't it instead reflect the state of programming jobs, where most of the frequent programmers are male?

Additionally, it is observed that women usually obtain their programming expertise through the formal education system. Unfortunately, formal educational institutions rarely have text-based coding included in their curriculums. Instead, it is more common to learn windows-oriented graphic coding environments such as Microsoft visual basic, visual C++ or Java. While coding for proprietary software is continuously reinforced, it is difficult for female programmers to be involved in FLOSS development that requires the skill of coding in a text based environment.

5) A lack of women-centred views in FLOSS development
The lack of female FLOSS developers results in a greater amount of female unfriendly software in the FLOSS system. Some scholars in science and technology studies (STS) have pointed out that technologies are gendered both in their design and use.**21** The social relations of gender within the FLOSS social world are reflected in and shaped by the design of FLOSS. The lack of women's perspectives on software design and use restricts women's participation in FLOSS development and, in turn, produces the stereotype that women are almost absent in FLOSS development because they are less able to program. This absence of female developers is a disadvantage for FLOSS development, and results in inequalities in an ICT-based society.

6) A male dominated competitive world view
> [The OSS market] is literally a war for the best and brightest. If we don't get there, somebody else will.
>> Andrew Clark, Director of strategy and market intelligence for the venture capital group at IBM**22**

As Arun and Arun point out, 'The project-based, competitive nature of software development reproduces a masculine culture, which further interacts with the different career patterns of women and social norms and tends to disadvantage

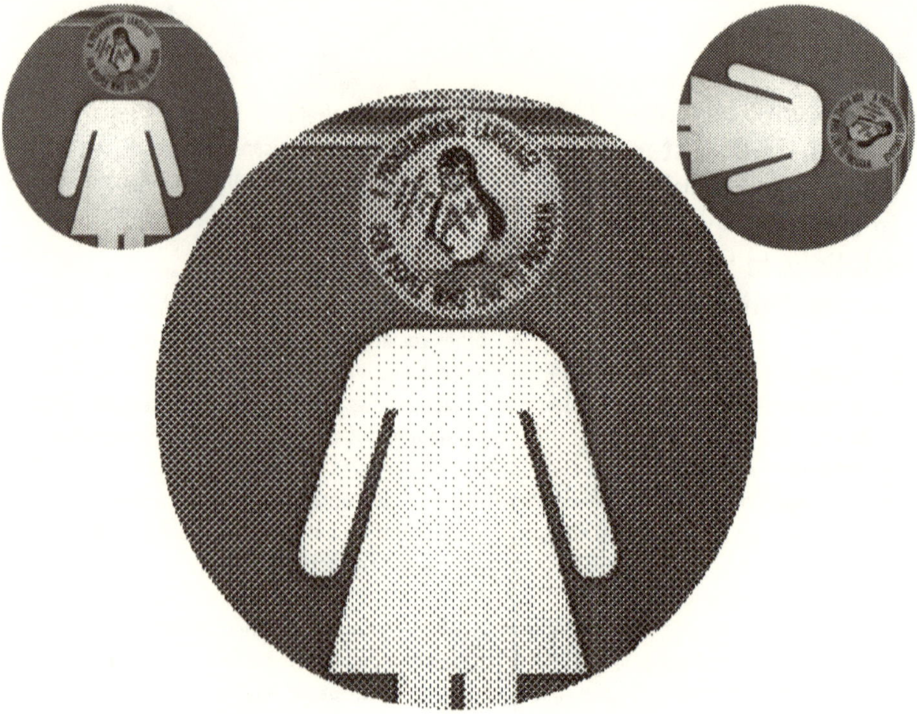

http://women.alioth.debian.org/

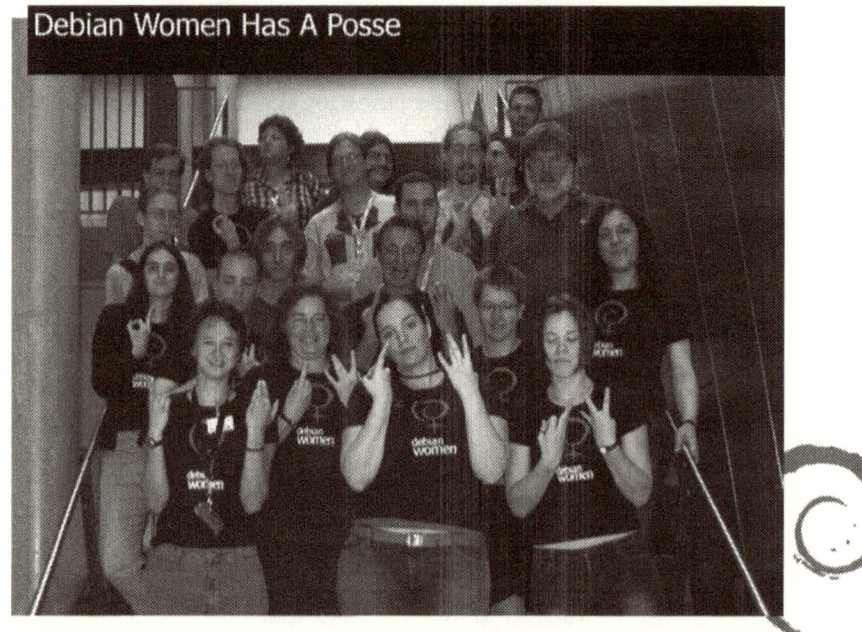

Debian Women Has A Posse

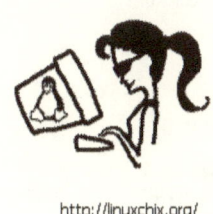

http://linuxchix.org/

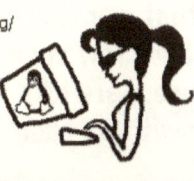

http://women.kde.org/

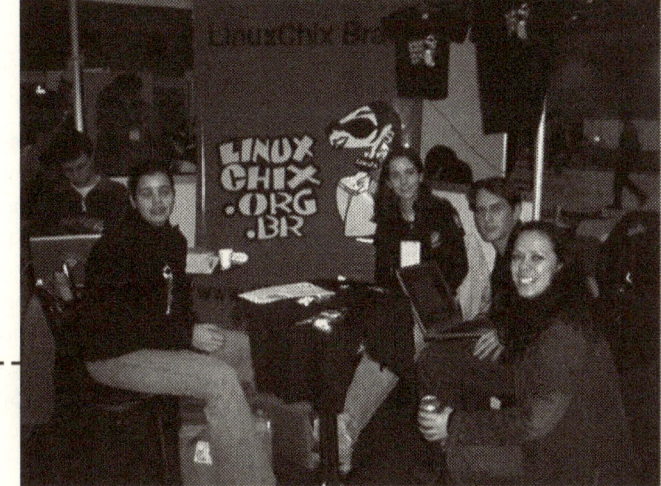

http://linuxchix.org.br/

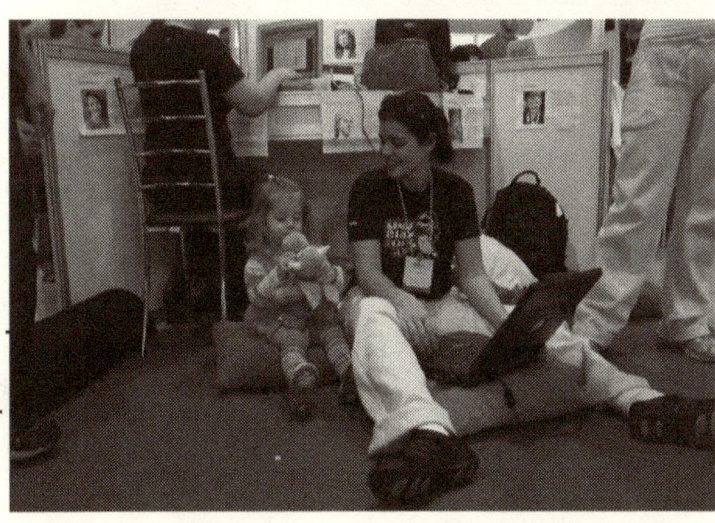

Collage :> Raquel Perez de Eulate

The text based nature of FLOSS programming means that women, who usually have few coding experiences, are less familiar with its operation

women.'**23** While statements in a similar tone to Clark's repeatedly surface in the mass media, the masculine competitive world view is continuously represented and reinforced in society. This carries over to the FLOSS social world, where more powerful, male members are generally in a position to determine and articulate the group's beliefs, practices, and interests. It is very alarming that on the whole the perspectives and purposes of FLOSS development are determined by white men.

HOW CAN/DOES FLOSS EMPOWER WOMEN?

There are three main objectives for the current 'women's movement' in the FLOSS community: 1) the provision of women friendly software and services; 2) the creation of a women friendly environment for developing and using FLOSS and; 3) the fostering of a gender balanced ICT innovation system for both competition and collaboration. These three points have close connections with one another - in order to create technology based products that engage and build on women's ideas and visions, we need to create a more women friendly environment in order to attract more women to participate in FLOSS development. Encompassing such a women centred view of design, which usually resembles a more sympathetic and inclusive way of doing things, will possibly foster a gender balanced ICT innovation system that is not only friendly to women but also to various minority groups. This system, unlike the current highly competitive approach, will draw on aptitudes and competences of diverse actors in the FLOSS social world so as to develop a holistic environment which is based on a collaborative approach.

Networking is important in 'democratising the access and dissemination of knowledge. In order to encourage women's participation and also to explain the operation of FLOSS to women, some female developers/users have started to network and form online groups such as, LinuxChix, KDE Women Gnurias, GenderChangers, and Debian-women.**24** They act to dispel the unfriendly wording in documents and, in online peer groups, to report sexist bug reports to other developers and give online tutorials. Networking and gathering, online or offline, can serve as a basis for gender inclusion.**25**

RESEARCH THE FUTURE!

It is anticipated that through conceptualising and documenting the current gender issues in FLOSS development, it will help enlarge the knowledge base for gender sensitive policies on ICTs, and propose a women centred policy towards developing and implementing FLOSS. While FLOSS represents a new milestone for software

The continuing production of *gendered* software and ICT products will only make the gender gap in ICT grow

development and knowledge production in a broad sense that might alter the social relations of gender,**26** 'in this technoscientifically advanced era, feminist politics make wider differences in the women-machine relationship than the technologies themselves'.**27** As such, a gender-sensitive agenda for developing FLOSS is urgently needed.

However, in speaking of implementing and developing FLOSS, most of the cases are centered on or situated in developed countries. One should bear in mind that there are many undocumented activities that have happened in the developing world. When strengthening the advantages of FLOSS, we should not overlook many problems emerging from implementing FLOSS in developing countries, such as a lack of sufficient training and support.**28** The digital divide must be considered as a symptom of inequality, not the cause of it. There is a need to understand what local people really need: water, food, jobs, decent healthcare and sanitation, or software and ICT infrastructures. ICT gender issue might be more complex than we have seen here. Female participants very often suffer from hybrid discriminations, both from the male-dominated FLOSS world and socio-cultural patriarchy, although virtual groups such Linuxchix Brazil and Linuxchix Africa have started providing women with help in solving problems in implementing Linux, more effort needs to be made in documenting, analysing and deconstructing the patriarchal hegemony embedded in the whole ICT infrastructure.**29** As such, like many other fields concerned with gendering, this essay is a mere beginning - an analytic stage on which 'we need to place the details contributed by ethnographic research, cultural critiques, sociological surveys, legal scholarship on men and women in their many specific conditions and subjectivities.'**30** ⚘

This is an edited version of the paper submitted for the encyclopedia *Gender and IT* http://genderitencyclopedia.ist.psu.edu to be published by IDEA Groups in 2006. This draft is released under the General Public Licence. The document itself has the potential to be improved in an open source culture. If you have comments or ideas on how it can be improved, please do not hesitate to contact me. Later the online version will then be adjusted to take account of these points

FOOTNOTES

1 See, Schuler, D. & Namioka, A. (eds.), *Participatory Design, Principles and Practices.* Hillsdale, NJ: Lawrence Erlbaum Associates, 1993; McBreen, P, 'Software Development: Dismantling the Waterfall', Boston, MA: Addison-Wesley, 2002 http://www.informit.com/articles/article.asp?p=25272; Norman, D. & Draper, S. (eds.), *User Centered System Design: New Perspectives on Human-Computer Interaction,* Hillsdale, NJ: Lawrence Erlbaum Associates, 1986 ; and http://www.extremeprogramming.org/ or http://www.xprogramming.com/; and, Beck, K., *Extreme Programming Explained: Embrace Change,* Boston, MA: Addison-Wesley, 1999

2 See, Ghosh, R.A. et al., 'Free/Libre and Open Source Software: survey and study. Deliverable D18: Final Report. Part IV: Survey of Developers' International Institute of Infonomics, University of Maastricht and Berlecon Research GmbH. The original version of this document is available at http://www.infonomics.nl/FLOSS/report/

3 See, Levesque M. & Wilson, G., 'Women in software: Open source, cold shoulder', Software Development, 2004 http://www.sdmagazine.com/documents/s=9411/sdm0411b/sdm0411b.html?temp=TgtgS9YUY8; and, Public report on the consultation meeting on European perspectives for open source software", ftp://ftp.cordis.lu/pub/ist/docs/ka4/tesss-OSS-report.pdf 2001

4 See, UNDP Bratislava Regional Center and UNIFEM Central and Eastern Europe, *Bridging the Gender Digital Divide: A Report on Gender and Information Communication Technologies (ICT) in Central and Eastern Europe and the Commonwealth of Independent States (CIS),* UNDP/UNIFEM, 2004

5 See, Mitter S. & Rowbotham, S. (eds.), *Women Encounter Technology: Changing Patterns of Employment in the Third World,* London: Routledge and The United Nations University, 1995

6 See, DeBare, Ilana, *Women in Computing: Logged On or Left Out?* A Sacramento Bee Special Report, Jan. 21, 1996

7 See, Bleier, R., 'Sex difference research: Science or Belief?' In R. Bleier (Ed.), *Feminist Approaches to Science.* New York: Teachers College Press, 1991, pp. 147-164

8 UK Equal Opportunities Commission, *Plugging Britain's Skills Gap: Challenging Gender Segregation in Training and Work,* Report of phase one of the EOC's investigation into gender segregation and modern apparenticeships. Equal Opportunities Commission, UK, 2004

9 http://www.iwt.org/systers.html

10 See, Walby, S. & Olsen, W., *The Impact of Women's Position in the Labour Market on Pay and Implications for Productivity,* Department of Trade and Industry Women and Equality Unit (WEU) funded research using the British Household Panel Survey, 2002

11 See, Walby, S., 'Segregation in employment in social and economic theory' in S. Walby (ed.) *Gender Segregation at Work.* Milton Keynes: Open University Press, 1988, pp. 14-28; Rubery, J. & Smith, M. & Fagan, C., *Women's Employment in Europe,* ch. 5 'Occupational Segregation', London: Routledge, 1999, pp. 168-222; and Miller, L. et al, *Occupational Segregation, Gender Gaps and Skill Gaps,* Manchester: Equal Opportunities Commission, 2004 www.eoc.org.uk

12 See, Lin, Y. *Hacking Practices and Software Development: A Social Worlds Analysis of ICT Innovation and the Role of Open Source Software,* 2004, Department of Sociology, University of York, UK. (Unpublished doctoral thesis)

13 Turkle, S. *The Second Self: Computers and the Human Spirit.* New York: Simon and Schuster, 1984

14 http://www.eriders.org

15 See, Okin, Susan Moller, 1999, http://www.bostonreview.net/BR22.5/okin.html

16 Ibid

17 Ibid

18 Ibid

19 Allison Randal is the president of the Perl Foundation and part of the core developers in the Perl 6 project. Amaya is a Debian GNU/Linux developer and one of the founders of Debian-Women group

20 Fieldwork at Italian Code Jam 2004, Ferrara, Italy: http://www.codejam.org/index.en.html

21 See, for example: Edwards, P, 'Gender and the Cultural Construction of Computing', adapted from 'From "Impact" to Social Process: Case Studies of Computers in Politics, Society, and Culture, Chapter IV-A,' *Handbook of Science and Technology Studies*, Beverly Hills: Sage Press; and, Wajcman, Judy, *TechnoFeminism*, Polity, 2004

22 From an interview with C|Net.com, February 14, 2005

23 Arun, S. & Arun, T. G, 'Gender at Work Within the Software Industry: An Indian Perspective', *Journal of Women and Minorities in science and engineering* 7(3), (2001)

24 http://www.linuxchix.org/, http://women.kde.org/, http://www.gnurias.org.br/, http://www.genderchangers.org/, http://women.alioth.debian.org/

25 See, Nordli, H., 'The Gathering Experience: A User study of a Computer Party' presented at the 'Strategies on Inclusion: Gender and the Information Society (SIGIS)" conference, 2004, http://www.rcss.ed.ac.uk/sigis/public/displaydoc/full/D05_2.1 2_NTNU1

26 Lin, Y. op. cit

27 See, Wajcman, op. cit.

28 *Guardian*, February 17, 2005. 'Bridging the digital divide', http://www.guardian.co.uk/online/story/0,3605,1415713,00.html

29 http://www.linuxchix.org.br, http://www.africalinuxchix.org

30 See, Sassen, S., *Blind Spots: Towards a Feminist Analytics of Today's Global Economy*, 1999, http://www.uwm.edu/Dept/IGS/presentation/sassen.pdf

Yuwei Lin <yuwei@ylin.org> is undertaking post-doctoral research into the social and cultural implications of science and technology, free/libre open source software (FLOSS) studies, and dynamics in virtual communities at the Vrije Universiteit Amsterdam, http://www.ylin.org

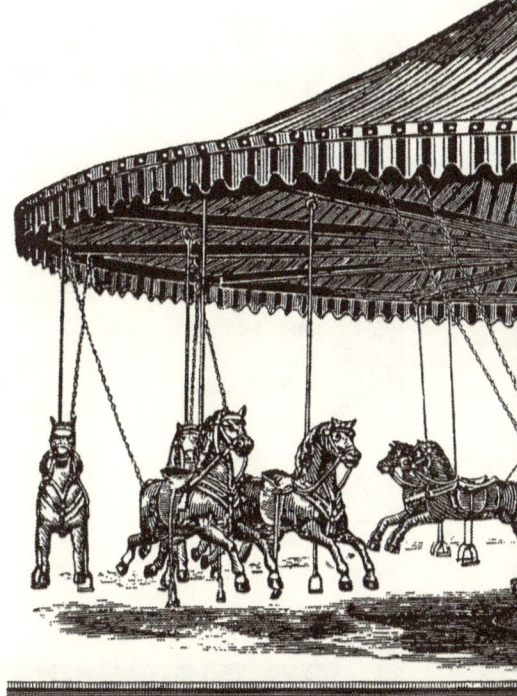

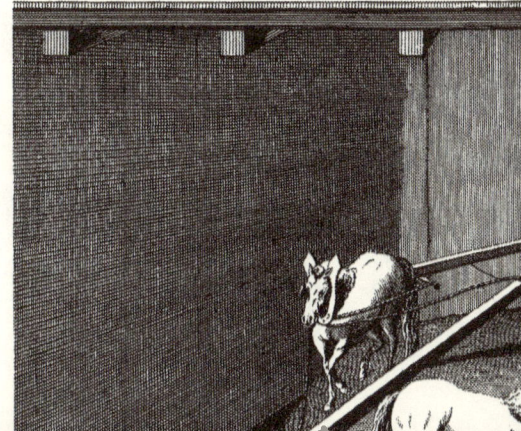

MUTE

CULTURE AND POLITICS AFTER THE NET

Subscription Rates

	individual		institutional/company	
	4 issues (1 year)	8 issues (2 years)	4 issues (1 year)	8 issues (2 years)
uk	£18	£34	£27	£51
eu	€25	€48	€38	€71
usa/can/mx	$22	$41	$32	$61
other	€29	€54	€43	€82

go to www.metamute.org/subs/

Subscriptions will start with the current issue,
unless otherwise specified in the 'special delivery instruc-
tions' field

GIFT SUBSCRIPTIONS:
If you are giving *Mute* to a friend, you can leave their details
on completion of your purchase together with your own pay-
ment details and a special gift card to them. This leaves you
free to add other items to your order

INSTITUTIONAL OPTIONS:
T: +44(0)20 7377 6949
F: +44(0)20 7377 9520
E: subs@metamute.org

ADDRESS CHANGE:
If you are an existing subscriber needing to change your
address, then please email us on subs@metamute.org

Web www.metamute.org/subs/
Email <subs@metamute.org>

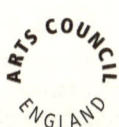

subscribe

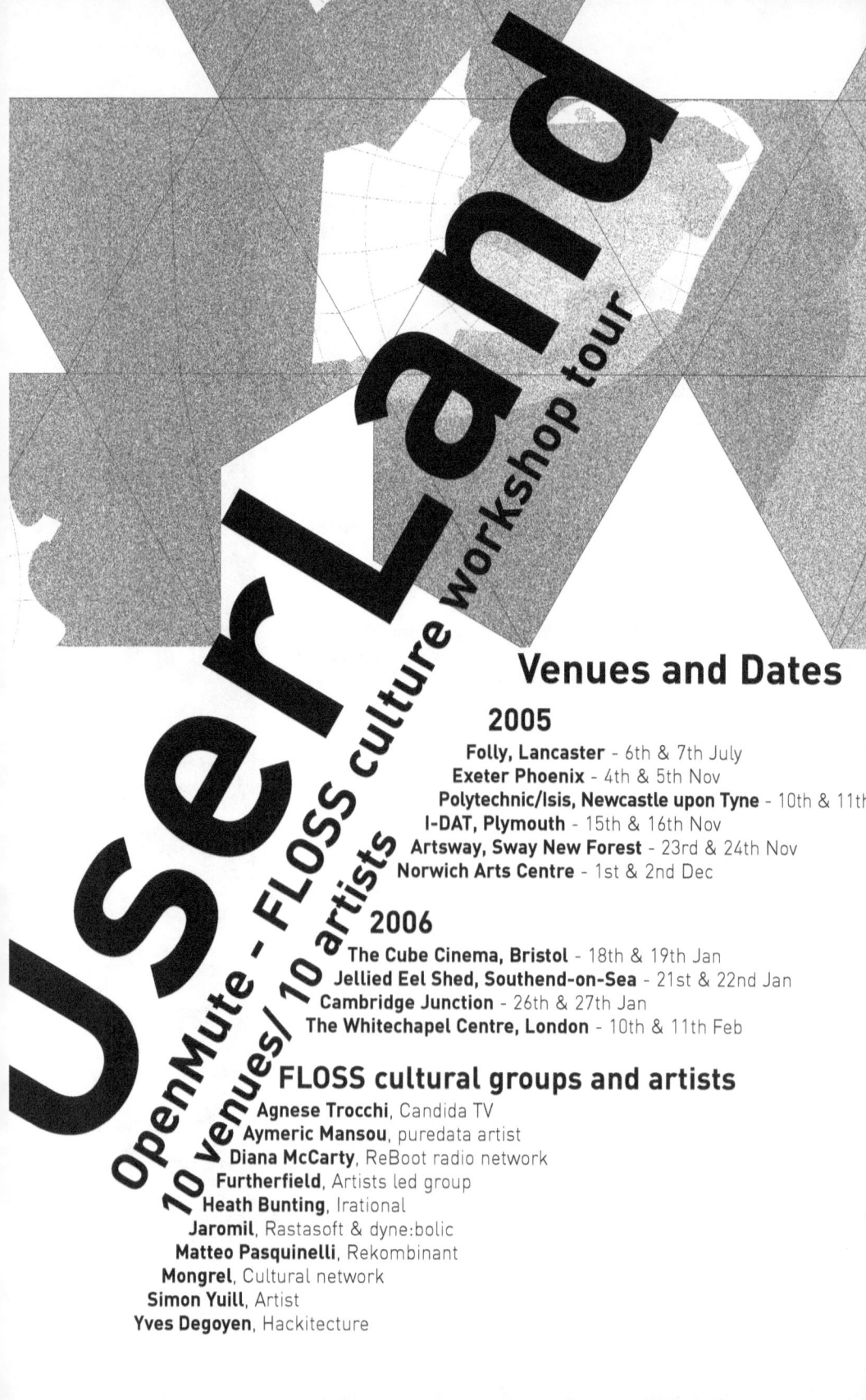

UserLand

OpenMute - FLOSS culture workshop tour

10 venues/ 10 artists

Venues and Dates

2005

Folly, Lancaster - 6th & 7th July
Exeter Phoenix - 4th & 5th Nov
Polytechnic/Isis, Newcastle upon Tyne - 10th & 11th
I-DAT, Plymouth - 15th & 16th Nov
Artsway, Sway New Forest - 23rd & 24th Nov
Norwich Arts Centre - 1st & 2nd Dec

2006

The Cube Cinema, Bristol - 18th & 19th Jan
Jellied Eel Shed, Southend-on-Sea - 21st & 22nd Jan
Cambridge Junction - 26th & 27th Jan
The Whitechapel Centre, London - 10th & 11th Feb

FLOSS cultural groups and artists

Agnese Trocchi, Candida TV
Aymeric Mansou, puredata artist
Diana McCarty, ReBoot radio network
Furtherfield, Artists led group
Heath Bunting, Irational
Jaromil, Rastasoft & dyne:bolic
Matteo Pasquinelli, Rekombinant
Mongrel, Cultural network
Simon Yuill, Artist
Yves Degoyen, Hackitecture

Go to **openmute.org** for
details and bookings

Organisers: OpenMute – FLOSS Application Service Provider (ASP)

Map artwork based on R. Buckminster Fuller's Dymaxion Air-Ocean World map ©1938.
Design – Damian Jaques and Simon Worthington – OpenMute

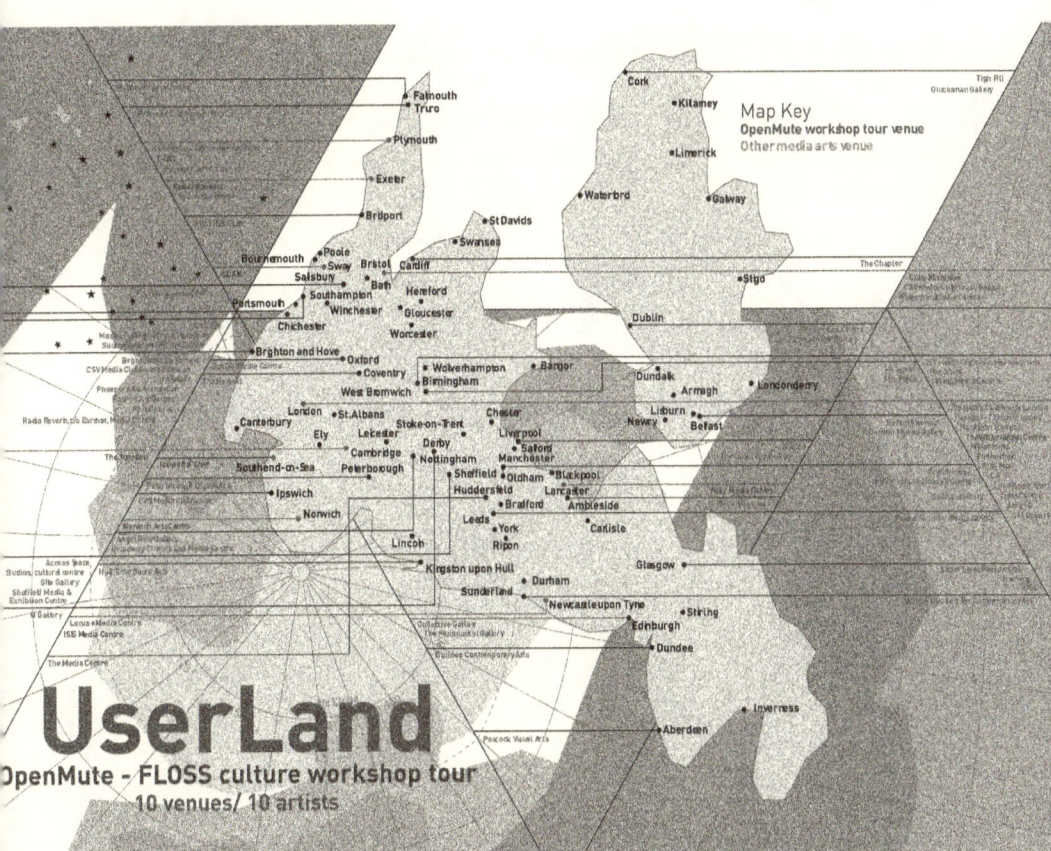

OM1 FREE SERVICES

Easily build or update your site with our browser based tools, create your group's online meeting place or your own individual information site

WHAT YOU GET

Tools

Add content to web pages, through news and galleries

Collaborate through forums and event calendars

Share files using downloads

Also included:

wiki (collaborative workspace), partners, links, members, headlines (RDF newsfeeds), polls and FAQ

Address

Choose your free web address:

http://yourname.omweb.org

Space

5MB web space, 5MB Gallery space, 20MB bandwidth per month

Support

OpenMute community support, online manuals, tutorials and FAQ

OpenMute and *Mute* are funded by Arts Council England

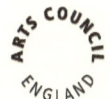

www.ingramcontent.com/pod-product-compliance
Lightning Source LLC
Chambersburg PA
CBHW030354290526
45785CB00004B/1739